ISBN 1-930596-37-5

Published by THE GUEST COTTAGE, INC.
PO Box 848
Woodruff, WI 54568
1-800-333-8122
www.theguestcottage.com

Designed and marketed by The Guest Cottage, Inc.
Cover art by Julie Bauknecht

Printed in U.S.A.

The
Guest
Cottage Inc.
dba Amherst Press

More Minnesota Mornings and Beyond

A Cookbook & Travel Guide

from the Minnesota

Bed & Breakfast Association

Minnesota
Bed & Breakfast
Association

Beyond Indeed!

It is with great intention that we use the word "beyond" in the title of this cookbook. We meant it to be more than breakfast recipes initially. You'll often experience afternoon snacks, a full cookie jar, and sometimes tea or evening appetizers for special holidays. Within some regions of our state, innkeepers work together promoting their area and offer tours of their inns with special treats during the holidays or to raise funds for a local cause. Many of the MBBA inns offer dinner, if their location or local ordinance allows.

But we encourage the reader to think about what "beyond" also means as it relates to a B & B experience. The thesaurus lists synonyms such as

- *remote and more remote*
- *farther*
- *free of*
- *outside*
- *past*
- *superior to*
- *without*
- *yonder*

Any one of these words would relate to a Minnesota B & B experience. Often traveling to a little out of the way inn, on a country road, passing through a town you may not have visited if it were not for this reservation certainly fits "remote" or "beyond". As innkeepers we certainly like to think your B & B experience will be "superior to" any other lodging opportunity available. That is one of the definitions we like best and strive to offer with fine food, comfy furniture, luxury "without" comparison and details, details, details. If we think of "beyond" as "free of" that too is B & B, such as "free of" noise, pollution, interruptions, traffic.

There is nothing that the Minnesota B & B Association members would like more than for you to come and enjoy their fine food and think "beyond"! Yes, bed and breakfast and beyond indeed! Travel through the pages herein and imagine "beyond" while cooking up one of the fun recipes inside and then come "yonder" and enjoy a time away and let us do the cooking for you. Beyond comparison! That's a Minnesota B & B and Beyond Experience.

Quality Assured Inn of the Minnesota Bed & Breakfast Association.
All Inns in our membership have successfully completed a review program
that recognizes standards of quality endorsed by the association in areas of
cleanliness, safety, guest comfort, and host professionalism and integrity.

Contents

Participating Inns

State Map of Participating Inns

Orr •

Ely •

Grand Marais •

• Grand Rapids

• Park Rapids

Duluth •

• Vergas
• Pelican Rapids

Fergus Falls • • Battle Lake

• Brainerd

• Alexandria

Taylors Falls
• Center City

Monticello •

Anoka •

St. Paul ◉ • Stillwater
Farmington •

Jordan • • Hastings

Red Wing •
Cannon Falls • • Lake City

• New Ulm

• Zumbrota

• Waseca

Winona •

Lanesboro •

N
W — E
S

Minnesota

Guide By City of Participating Inns

Cedar Rose Inn

422 7th Avenue West
Alexandria, MN 56308
(320)762-8430
(888)203-5333
www.cedarroseinn.com
aggie@cedarroseinn.com

Hosts: Florian & Aggie Ledermann

The Cedar Rose Inn Bed & Breakfast offers all the comforts of home, whether you're looking for a romantic escape, a historically unique home or a place to kick up your feet while on a hectic business trip. Located in the "Silk Stocking District" near downtown Alexandria, the Inn is within walking distance of many antique shops and restaurants. You will be greeted by beds of blooming roses as you drive up the circular driveway to the front porch. When you arrive, a crackling fireplace and a visit to our special infrared sauna will warm your heart. Guests marvel at the spacious, quiet bedrooms, all four with private baths and two with whirlpools.

Rates at Cedar Rose Inn range from $85 to $140.
Rates include a full breakfast.

Ham & Cheese Egg Bake

This recipe is sure to please! The frosted corn flakes give the dish added flavor and crunch. You need to prepare this the night before you're planning on serving it.

Serves 8-10

16 slices bread
2 cups ham
8 ounces Swiss cheese
8 ounces Cheddar cheese
6 eggs
3 cups milk
1/2 teaspoon onion salt
1/2 teaspoon dry mustard

Topping:
3 cups crushed frosted corn flakes
1/2 cup butter
*Mix flakes and melted butter together.
Sprinkle on top just before baking.*

1 medium mixing bowl
9" x 13" baking pan

Baking Time: 45 minutes
Baking Temperature: 350°

Trim crust from bread and fill bottom of baking pan with half of the bread. Layer ham and cheese and second layer of bread. In a medium mixing bowl, mix milk, eggs and seasoning; pour over bread. Refrigerate overnight.

Remove from refrigerator 1 hour before baking. Preheat oven to 350°. Sprinkle frosted flake mixture over top and bake for 45 minutes.

Wild Rice & Sausage Quiche

Wild rice is abundant in Minnesota, so it seems only appropriate to present a dish with ties to the state. This quiche is quick, simple and simply delicious!

Makes 6-8 servings

      1   package (12 ounces) Jimmy Dean sausage
      1   small onion, diced
           9" unbaked pie shell
      1   cup shredded Monterey Jack cheese
      1   cup cooked wild rice
      3   eggs
  1-1/2   cups half-and-half
    1/2   teaspoon salt
           dash hot pepper sauce

           skillet
      1   medium mixing bowl

           Baking Time: 50 minutes
           Baking Temperature: 360°

   Preheat oven to 360°. Fry sausage and onion until onion is translucent. Drain and spread mixture evenly in pie shell. Sprinkle with cheese and cooked wild rice. In a medium mixing bowl, whip eggs, half-and-half, salt and pepper sauce. Pour over wild rice. Bake for 50 minutes or until center is set.

Raspberry Cheesecake Bars

This recipe may take a little more time to complete, but it is definitely worth the effort! You can store the extras, if there are any (!), in the refrigerator for up to 1 week, or they may frozen for up to 3 months.

Makes 32 bars

1-1/4	cups all-purpose flour
1/2	cup packed brown sugar
1/2	cup finely chopped almonds
1/2	cup butter
2	packages (8 ounces each) cream cheese, softened
2/3	cup granulated sugar
2	eggs
3/4	teaspoon almond extract
1	cup raspberry preserves
1/2	cup flaked coconut
1/2	cup sliced almonds
2	medium mixing bowls
	9" x 13" x 2" baking pan

Baking Time: 42-45 minutes, divided
Baking Temperature: 350°

Preheat oven to 350°. Grease the baking pan; set aside. In a medium mixing bowl, combine flour, brown sugar and chopped almonds. Cut in butter until mixture resembles fine crumbs. Set aside 1/2 cup of crumb mixture for topping. For crust, press remaining crumb mixture into the bottom of prepared pan. Bake for 12-15 minutes or until edges are golden.

While crust is baking, in a medium mixing bowl, beat cream cheese, granulated sugar, eggs and almond extract until smooth. Spread over hot crust. Return to oven and bake for 15 minutes or until edges of crust are lightly browned.

Spread preserves over cream cheese mixture. In a small mixing bowl, combine the reserved crumb mixture, coconut and sliced almonds. Sprinkle mixture over preserves. Return pan to oven and bake for 15 minutes more. Cool in pan on a wire rack. Chill for 3 hours before cutting.

Ticknor Hill
Bed & Breakfast

**1625 Third Avenue
Anoka, MN 55303
(763)421-9687
(800)484-3954 ext. 6391
www.ticknorhill.com
d1wallace@yahoo.com**

Hosts: Dave & Debbie Wallace

Ticknor Hill Bed & Breakfast was built in 1867 in the bustling river town of Anoka. It is listed on the National Register of Historic Homes. Today, the town still reflects the charm and hospitality of yesteryear. The Inn, with its spacious guest rooms and common areas, invites you to relax. As guests, you are welcome to enjoy the peacefulness of the porches, the warmth of the fireplaces in your room, the library or the parlor, the sunshine streaming in the conservatory or a game of billiards. A bountiful breakfast is served daily in our elegant dining room or a private breakfast is available upon request. Each of our guest rooms is uniquely decorated with a king or queen-size bed, private bathroom, fireplace, and window air conditioning. Our Ticknor Suite and Wilkens Room have a double whirlpool tub.

We are located within walking distance of the riverfront, several antique stores, restaurants, coffee shops, live theater and unique gift galleries. Nearby you will find golf courses, hiking, biking and cross-country ski trails. Sporting events, the Twin Cities and the Mall of America are only a short drive away.

Rates at Ticknor Hill Bed & Breakfast range from $110 to $150.
Rates include a full breakfast.

Chicken Pockets

This is a signature dish we serve to luncheon guests. It's tasty and easy to prepare and serve.

Makes 4 pockets

  3 ounces cream cheese, softened
  2 Tablespoons melted margarine or butter
  2 cups chicken, cooked and cut into small pieces
1/2 teaspoon seasoned salt
  2 Tablespoons milk
  1 Tablespoon chopped onion or chives
  1 Tablespoon chopped pimento, optional
  1 can (8 ounces) refrigerated crescent roll dough
  2 Tablespoons melted margarine or butter
     Italian bread crumbs
     Parmesan cheese

     mixer
  1 medium mixing bowl
     baking sheets
     roller
     pastry brush

Baking Time: 20-25 minutes
Baking Temperature: 350°

Preheat oven to 350°. In a medium mixing bowl, blend together cream cheese and melted margarine. Add chicken, seasoned salt, milk, onion and pimento.

Separate crescent rolls. Make 4 rectangles and seal on the dotted lines.

Put 1/2 cup mixture on to each rectangle and bring up edges together in center. Brush with melted margarine or butter. Sprinkle with Italian bread crumbs and Parmesan cheese.

Bake for 20-25 minutes.

Xanadu Island
Bed & Breakfast and Resort

35484 235th Street
Battle Lake, MN 56515
(218)864-8096
(800)396-9043
www.xanadu.cc
xanadu@prtel.com

Hosts: Bryan & Janet Lonski

*X*anadu Island Bed & Breakfast and Resort is located on a private secluded island in West Central Minnesota. The main lodge was built in 1920 by a wealthy Missouri industrialist who built it as a "fishing shack" for his millionaire friends from the East. The Fargo Forum later referred to it as a "mansion." Guests now are able to experience a serene, peaceful getaway in a beautiful setting. The lodge features massive stone fireplaces, private baths and double Jacuzzis. Also nestled among the oaks and maples on the island are 3 cottages, which were originally the servants' quarters. A canoe, paddle boat, fishing boats, campfire ring and hammocks all entice guests to relax and linger a while.

Rates at Xanadu Island Bed & Breakfast and Resort range from $95 to $155.
Rates include a full breakfast.

Cheese Bake

This cheese bake was discovered by Bryan at a time when Janet was off supervising a newly arrived grandchild. It is easy to prepare the night before, so you can just pop it in the oven an hour before breakfast. It is particularly popular when served with fresh pecan rolls and a breakfast meat.

Serves 4

- 8 ounces Monterey Jack cheese
- 4 eggs
- 1/2 cup milk
- 1 teaspoon sugar
- 1/4 cup flour
- 1 teaspoon baking powder
- 2 ounces cubed cream cheese
- 8 ounces cottage cheese
- 3 Tablespoons melted butter

1 large mixing bowl
9" square baking dish

**Baking Time: 45 minutes;
60 minutes if refrigerated overnight
Baking Temperature: 325°**

In a large mixing bowl, beat eggs, milk and sugar. Add flour and baking powder. Continue beating and adding remainder of ingredients. Spray baking dish with nonstick cooking spray. Pour mixture into baking dish. You may refrigerate overnight or bake uncovered in a preheated 325° oven for 45 minutes. If refrigerated overnight, adjust baking time to 60 minutes.

Whiteley Creek Homestead Bed & Breakfast

12349 Whiteley Creek Trail
Brainerd, MN 56401
(218)829-0654
www.whiteleycreek.com
whiteleycrk@aol.com

Host: Adrienne Cahoon

Each evening, guests may gather in twig chairs around a crackling fire that blazes in a huge fieldstone fireplace on the back porch while enjoying a dessert and beverage. In the morning, guests are served breakfast in the Kindred Spirits Tearoom, an 1890 railroad coach car, furnished with antique kitchen utensils and vintage aprons. Themed Inn rooms, "Starry, Starry Night" and "Miss 4th of July," have private baths and unique décor. Guests may cozy up to the fireplace in the "Three Marigolds and One Other Flower" cottage, to the rear of an old-fashioned general store with 1930-40s cars and trucks parked outside beside an antique gas pump. In the "Out My Kitchen Window" barn cottage, a loft with French doors opens onto a balcony overlooking acres of land. A fireplace is on the lower level to take the chill out of the evening air. The cozy "Cabin In The Pines" cottage is snuggled amongst the pines. Relive the past at Whiteley Creek and go back to a time when clothes swung lazily on a line in the breeze.

Rates at Whiteley Creek Bed & Breakfast range from $85 to $110.
Rates include a full breakfast.

Flossie's Eggs on the Rails

Fragrant rosemary and curry from our herb garden partner to give the classics eggs benedict a new twist. Flossie, Whiteley Creek's prolific egg layer, dutifully supplies the main ingredient for this flavorful entrée served in an 1890 railroad car.

Serves 4

4 slices white bread	4 custard cups or measuring cups
2 Tablespoons olive oil	saucepan
2 sprigs fresh rosemary leaves, chopped	large pan for poaching eggs
sea salt	baking sheet
freshly ground pepper	
2 teaspoons white distilled vinegar	
1/4 teaspoon salt	
4 large eggs	
4 slices corned beef	
paprika	

Preheat oven on broiler setting. Fill a large pan with 2" of water and bring to boil. Add vinegar and salt. Reduce heat to low.

While water is heating, lightly brush one side of each bread slice with olive oil. Sprinkle with sea salt and pepper. Place slices with olive oil side down on baking sheet. Broil in oven until lightly toasted. Flip slices over and sprinkle with rosemary. Return to oven to toast. Wrap toast in aluminum foil to keep warm.

Break eggs into separate custard cups. Slide eggs into water so eggs keep their shape when they hit the water. Cook for 5 minutes. Use a slotted spoon to lift eggs out of water and place them on a paper towel to drain.

Put a slice of bread on each plate. Top with a slice of corned beef and a poached egg. Drizzle with warm curry sauce (below). Sprinkle with paprika.

Curry Sauce:
      1 can (10.75 ounces) cream of chicken soup *(not reduced sodium or fat)*
   1/2 cup milk *(may need a little more for thinning)*
   1/4 teaspoon curry powder
1-1/2 teaspoons freshly squeezed lemon juice

In saucepan, combine all ingredients. Heat until warm. Sauce recipe yield 7 servings.

Quill and Quilt

615 Hoffman Street West
Cannon Falls, MN 55009
(507)263-5507
(800)488-3849
www.QuillandQuilt.com
info@QuillandQuilt.com

Hosts: Matt & Rachel Gillen

In 1897, Dr. A.T. Conley, a physician in Cannon Falls for over 40 years, built this grand three-story home. Our home is a classic example of Colonial Revival architecture. Join us in the parlor, in front of the tiger oak striped fireplace with Italian porcelain tile. Peruse our collection of books, magazines, DVD movies and games. Five cozy rooms make up our guest accommodations. Most rooms feature a fireplace and a Jacuzzi tub. Our third floor boasts the spa suite, which offers full body massage and specialty spa treatments by appointment. One block from the Inn you will find the Cannon River Winery, the Cannon Valley Bike Trail and the Cannon River!

Please see our website for a tour of the Inn, specials and hot deals: www.QuillandQuilt.com.

Rates at Quill and Quilt range from $79 to $189.
Rates include a full or continental breakfast.

Fresh Strawberry Soup

*This refreshing, chilled soup is delightful on a summer day but tastes delicious anytime.
Berries that are a little past their prime make a much more flavorful soup. It can be made
a couple of days in advance and frozen. Put it in the refrigerator the night before.*

Makes 10 half-cup servings

5 **cups washed, cleaned and hulled strawberries**
1/3 **cup sugar**
1 **Tablespoon Amaretto**
1-1/2 **cups whipping cream**
1/2 **teaspoon cinnamon**

blender or smoothie machine
measuring cups and spoons

Put cleaned, hulled strawberries in blender. Puree for 1 minute. Add
remaining ingredients. Blend until mixture looks like buttermilk, then
pulse a few times to be sure all ingredients are well blended.

Store in refrigerator overnight or in freezer up to one month. Allow to
thaw overnight before serving.

Topping:
1 **can (7 ounces) Redi Whip®**
 small bunch mint leaves, rinsed
5 **sliced strawberries**

For serving, place a dollop of Redi Whip® on top, with a mint leaf for
garnish.

Place one or two strawberry slices in whipped cream, next to mint
leaf, for garnish.

Summit Inn
Bed & Breakfast

**208 Summit Avenue
P.O. Box 264
Center City, MN 55012
(651)257-4987
www.summitinn.us
crocus@mycidco.com**

Host: Elaine Sommer

Located among stately historic homes, high on a bluff overlooking a pristine lake where eagles and sunsets rule, the Summit Inn offers guests a unique combination of tranquility and history. Welcome to a slower, more peaceful pace of a bygone era.

Wake up slowly to coffee, fresh flowers and the smells of a sumptuous breakfast. Later, explore the community immortalized by "The Emigrants" and "Grumpy Old Men." Visit an award-winning winery or scout the numerous local antique stores. Join us at the Summit Inn and make yourself at home.

Rates at Summit Inn Bed & Breakfast range from $85 to $175.
Rates include a full breakfast.

Dr. Gunz's Cure-All Rhubarb Custard Pie

The original resident of this historical 100-year-old home, Dr. Gunz, was a firm believer in the homeopathic remedy of baking with love. This pie has been known to cure everything from scraped knees to broken hearts. To enhance the healing properties of this pie, use rhubarb freshly harvested from the backyard garden.

Makes 6-8 servings

 2 **9" pastry shells, unbaked**
1-3/4 **cup sugar**
 1/2 **cup flour**
 1/2 **teaspoon salt**
 2 **eggs, slightly beaten**
 6 **cups rhubarb, cut into 1/4" slices or 6 cups frozen rhubarb, thawed**
 2 **Tablespoons butter**

 1 **large mixing bowl**
   9" diameter pie plate

Baking Time: 15 minutes plus 45-60 minutes
Baking Temperature: 425°, then 350°

Preheat oven to 425°. Wash and slice rhubarb. Fit pastry shell into 9" pie plate.

In a large mixing bowl, combine flour, salt, eggs and sugar. Stir in rhubarb slices and mix well. Pour into unbaked pastry shell. Dot the top with butter. Cover with remaining pastry shell and crimp edges together with fingers. Cut slits into top crust in a decorative pattern, if you wish. (I usually draw a daisy.)

Bake for 15 minutes, then turn heat down to 350° and bake an additional 45-60 minutes or until pie filling bubbles out of slits on top and rhubarb is very soft. If top crust browns too quickly, tent a piece of aluminum foil over top of pie and continue baking until done.

Cool at least 1 hour before serving. Store in refrigerator.

Another great recipe from Summit Inn Bed & Breakfast:

Swedish Raspberry Almond Bars

Center City is the home of the first Swedish settlement in Minnesota. These bars incorporate some of the traditional flavors found in this cuisine. Homemade raspberry jam and an almond flavored topping ensure that these bars disappear quickly. Special guests might find these treats delicately served on a silver tray on their bedside table for a decadent evening treat.

Makes 4 dozen bars

1 cup butter, softened
1/2 cup sugar
2-1/2 cups flour
2/3 cup raspberry jam

1 medium mixing bowl
mixer
large cookie sheet

Baking Time: 25-30 minutes
Baking Temperature: 325°

Preheat oven to 325°. In a medium mixing bowl, cream butter and sugar. Add 2 cups flour and mix. Gradually stir in remaining flour, a Tablespoon at a time (may not need entire 1/2 cup if mixture gets too dry to stick together.)

Shape into 4 long rolls on ungreased cookie sheet. Indent the center of each roll using the edge of your hand. Spread indentation area with raspberry jam. Bake for 25-30 minutes or until very lightly browned.

Frosting:
1 cup powdered sugar
2 teaspoons almond extract
2-3 teaspoons hot water *(enough to make it easy to drizzle on bars)*

In a medium mixing bowl, mix powdered sugar and almond extract. Add hot water a teaspoonful at a time until mixture is easy to drizzle with a spoon. Frost while bars are hot, drizzling frosting over raspberry jam.

Cut into angles while still warm.

"Proper Teas" Apricot & White Chocolate Scones

These are the type of pastries served by local attorney and 50-year resident of the Summit Inn, S. Bernhard Wennerberg, when he was discussing political aspirations over "proper tea" with visiting state dignitaries.

Makes 16-20 pieces, about 6-8 servings

3 cups flour	*Topping:*
1/3 cup sugar	1 Tablespoon cream
2-1/2 teaspoons baking powder	2 Tablespoons sugar
1/2 teaspoon baking soda	*Spread top of scones with cream and*
3/4 teaspoon salt	*then sprinkle with sugar prior to baking.*
3/4 cup firm butter, cut into small pieces	
1/2 cup chopped dried apricots	1 medium mixing bowl
1/2 cup good quality white chocolate chunks	baking sheet
	pastry blender or fork
1 cup buttermilk	
	Baking Time: 12 minutes
	Baking Temperature: 450°

Preheat oven to 450°. In a medium mixing bowl, stir together flour, sugar, baking powder, baking soda and salt. Cut the butter into the flour mixture using a pastry blender or fork until the mixture resembles cornmeal. Stir in dried apricots and white chocolate.

Make a well in the center of the flour-butter mixture; add buttermilk all at once. Stir the mixture with a fork until dough pulls away from sides of bowl. Gather dough into a ball.

Turn out onto a slightly floured board. Pat to 1/2" thickness. Cut into small triangles. Spread top of scones with cream and then sprinkle with sugar. Bake on greased cookie sheet for 12 minutes or until golden brown. Serve warm.

A.G. Thomson House

2617 East Third Street
Duluth, MN 55812
(218)724-3464
(877)807-8077
www.thomsonhouse.biz
info@thomsonhouse.biz

Host: Bill Brakken

Situated high on a hillside in Duluth's historic mansion district, the A.G. Thomson House features expansive views of Lake Superior from its sun-drenched dining room, along with many of its guest rooms. The elegant 1909 Inn features seven spacious guest rooms with private baths, double whirlpool tubs and gas fireplaces. Ideally located on over an acre of park-like grounds in a quiet, secluded neighborhood, the historic Bed & Breakfast is just seven blocks from Duluth's Lakewalk and five minutes from downtown and the Canal Park entertainment district.

The Thomson House was recently voted one the Top 15 B&Bs in the U.S. for "Best Breakfast in the Great Plains" (*Arrington's Bed and Breakfast Journal* 2006 Book of Lists). Similar awards for the previous three years include "Best Weekend Escape," "Best in the Midwest," and "Most Privacy."

Rates at A.G. Thomson House range from $129 to $299.
Rates include a full breakfast.

Apple & Raisin Baskets with Rum Cream

Autumn at the A.G. Thomson House is a time for incorporating the bounty of the apple harvest in our breakfast menu. This recipe helps set the mood for a crisp fall day as guests awaken to the spiced aroma of simmering apples while watching the sun rise over Lake Superior.

Serves 6

6 puff pastry shells	*Rum Cream:*
6-8 medium Cortland or equivalent baking apple	1/2 pint heavy whipping cream
1/4 cup raisins	1/4 teaspoon rum flavoring
1/2 cup apple or cranberry-apple juice	*With an electric mixer, whip the cream until soft peaks form. Fold the rum flavoring into the whipped cream.*
1/4 cup packed brown sugar	
1-1/2 teaspoons cinnamon	
1/4 teaspoon nutmeg	cookie sheet
3 whole cloves	1 medium saucepan
1/2 cup chopped walnuts	
dried cranberries, for garnish	
cinnamon sticks, for garnish	

Bake puff pastry shells according to directions on package. Remove and save tops. Scoop out insides and discard dough. Set hollow shells aside.

Slice and core unpeeled apples. Place the apples, raisins, juice, brown sugar, cinnamon, nutmeg and cloves in a saucepan and cook over medium-high heat. Bring to a boil and reduce heat, stirring occasionally. Cook until apples are soft but still retain shape. Before serving, add walnuts.

Assemble by filling puff pastry shells with apple mixture. Place top back on shell. Top with rum cream. Garnish with dried cranberries and cinnamon sticks.

The Ellery House

28 South 21st Avenue East
Duluth, MN 55812
(218)724-7639
(800)355-3794 (ElleryH)
www.ElleryHouse.com
info@elleryhouse.com

Hosts: Jim & Joan Halquist

The Ellery House is a classic Victorian (1890) haven of quiet comfort and gracious hospitality near the Lake Superior Lakewalk in Duluth. Voted one of the "Best in the Midwest" by *Arrington's B & B Journal*, we are renowned for our tradition of unobtrusive pampering and memorable breakfasts.

Rates at the Ellery House range from $99 to $169.
Rates include a full breakfast.

Strawberry Rhubarb Muffins

Whether our guests enjoy an intimate breakfast in bed or join other guests in the dining room, our strawberry rhubarb muffins are always a favorite. We often serve them with Featherbed Eggs and our signature fresh fruit platter.

Makes 12 muffins

1/2 cup sugar	*Icing:*
1-3/4 cups flour	2 cups powdered sugar
2-1/2 teaspoons baking powder	4-6 Tablespoons half-and-half
3/4 teaspoon salt	1/2 teaspoon vanilla
1 egg, slightly beaten	*Mix together all ingredients until the*
3/4 cup plain yogurt (milk may be substituted)	*icing has a smooth, thin consistency.*
1/3 cup vegetable oil	1 large mixing bowl
1/2 teaspoon vanilla	1 small mixing bowl
3/4 cup diced fresh rhubarb	muffin pan
1 cup chopped fresh strawberries	
	Baking Time: 20-25 minutes
	Baking Temperature: 400°

Preheat oven to 400°. In a large mixing bowl, mix sugar, flour, baking powder and salt. In a small mixing bowl, combine egg, yogurt, oil and vanilla. Stir egg mixture into flour mixture just until all ingredients are moistened. Fold rhubarb and strawberries into batter.

Divide batter evenly between 12 greased muffin cups. Bake for 20-25 minutes or until golden brown.

Glaze warm muffins with icing.

Featherbed Eggs

Whether our guests enjoy an intimate breakfast in bed or join other guests in the dining room, Featherbed Eggs are always a favorite. We often serve them with Strawberry Rhubarb Muffins and our signature fresh fruit platter. This recipe is made the night before you plan to serve it.

Serves 2

- 2 **slices country French bread, 3/4" thick**
- 1 **cup diced ham**
- 1 **cup extra sharp, aged Cheddar cheese, grated**
- 3 **eggs** *(we recommend local farm fresh eggs)*
- 5/8 **cup half-and-half** *(eggs and half-and-half should equal 1 cup)*
- **pepper, freshly ground**

- 1 **quart casserole dish**
- 1 **small mixing bowl**
- **measuring cup**

Baking Time: 45 minutes
Baking Temperature: 350°

Place one layer of country French bread in buttered casserole dish so that the bottom is covered. Tuck in bread pieces to fill any spaces. Cover with grated cheese. Sprinkle with ham.

Mix eggs and half-and-half in a small mixing bowl. Mixture should make 1 cup of liquid. Drizzle mixture over top of cheese and ham. Grate pepper over the top.

Cover and refrigerate overnight.

Put in cold oven and turn oven to 350°. Bake uncovered for about 45 minutes until puffy and lightly golden.

Minnesota Chocolate Cake with Cream Cheese Frosting

There is no better way to wind up the day than sharing Minnesota Chocolate Cake with someone you love.

Makes 12 sharing-size pieces

2 cups unbleached flour	1 medium mixing bowl
1-1/2 cups white sugar	1 large mixing bowl
1/2 cup unsweetened baking cocoa	9" x 13" cake pan
1 teaspoon salt	Baking Time: 30 minutes
1 Tablespoon baking soda	Baking Temperature: 350°
1 cup buttermilk	
1 cup espresso or strong coffee	
2/3 cup oil	
1 egg	
1 teaspoon vanilla	

In a large mixing bowl, mix flour, sugar, salt and soda together. Add buttermilk, coffee, oil, egg and vanilla. Beat until batter is smooth and thin. Pour into greased cake pan.

Bake for about 30 minutes or until cake tests done with a toothpick. Cool before frosting.

Cream Cheese Frosting:

        8 ounces cream cheese
        4 Tablespoons soft, sweet butter
        1 teaspoon vanilla extract
    2 – 2-1/2 cups powdered sugar
        juice from 1/2 lemon

In a medium mixing bowl, combine cream cheese, butter, vanilla extract and powdered sugar; beat until smooth and creamy. Beat in lemon juice. (Do not add lemon juice earlier as it will curdle the cream cheese.)

Adjust flavorings to taste.

Frost cooled Minnesota Chocolate Cake.

The Firelight Inn on Oregon Creek

2211 East Third Street
Duluth, MN 55812
(218)724-0272
(888)724-0273
www.firelightinn.com
info@firelightinn.com

Hosts: Jim & Joy Fischer

The Firelight Inn on Oregon Creek is a luxury Bed & Breakfast in Duluth. We welcome you to be pampered with comfortable accommodations and the finest amenities! Each suite features a gas fireplace, state-of-the-art air conditioning, Jacuzzi whirlpools for two, private bathrooms, TV/VCR/DVD, audio system and CD player. Our specialty is delivering your full, delicious breakfast to your suite each morning, which can be eaten by the firelight in the privacy of your suite. You may choose to dine on an outdoor deck, in the glass-enclosed front porch of the Inn, or we would be happy to serve you in the formal dining room.

The Inn is located on a secluded, dead-end street adjacent to Oregon Creek and amidst turn-of-the-century mansions in the historic East End of Duluth. Only two and one-half hours north of the Mall of America, about twenty blocks from historic downtown Duluth and seven blocks uphill from Lake Superior, the property offers peace and relaxation, an elegant setting and luxurious accommodations. We are proud members of Select Registry, Distinguished Inns of North America. "Let the warmth of the firelight surround you!"

Rates at The Firelight Inn on Oregon Creek range from $179 to $279.
Rates include a full breakfast.

Savory Croissant Breakfast Pudding

Your guest may hear you "bam" as you prepare this special breakfast entrée and will delight in this light and tasty breakfast pudding served with fresh fruit and a coffee cake.

Serves 8-10

2 Tablespoons unsalted butter, divided
1 cup finely chopped yellow onions
1/4 cup finely chopped green bell peppers
1/4 cup finely chopped red bell peppers
3/4 teaspoon salt, divided
1/4 teaspoon freshly ground black pepper, divided
2 teaspoons minced garlic
1 Tablespoon minced fresh parsley
6 ounces Canadian bacon, trimmed and diced
6 ounces breakfast sausage, crumbled or chopped
8 large eggs
3 cups whole milk
1/2 cup heavy cream
1-1/4 teaspoon Emeril's Original Essence, divided
8 cups torn, stale croissants (about 8 croissants)
8 ounces grated Gouda cheese (about 2 cups)

Topping:
1/2 cup fine, dry bread crumbs (croissants)
1/2 cup freshly grated Parmesan cheese
2 Tablespoons melted, unsalted butter
Emeril's Original Essence

In a small mixing bowl, combine bread crumbs, cheese, butter and remaining 1/2 teaspoon essence.

9" x 13" baking dish
measuring utensils
medium skillet
1 small mixing bowl
1 large mixing bowl

Baking Time: 75 minutes
Baking Temperature: 350° and 375°

Preheat oven to 350°. Lightly grease baking dish with 1 Tablespoon butter and set aside. In a medium skillet, melt 2 Tablespoons butter over medium high heat. Add onions, green and red peppers, 1/4 teaspoon salt and 1/8 teaspoon pepper ; cook, stirring until soft, about 3 minutes. Add garlic and cook, stirring until fragrant, about 30 seconds. Add parsley, stir and remove from heat. Let cool.

In a medium skillet, melt remaining 1 teaspoon butter over medium high heat. Add Canadian bacon and cook, stirring for 3 minutes. Drain on paper towels. Add sausage to skillet and cook, stirring until browned, about 5 minutes. Drain on paper towels.

In a large bowl, beat eggs. Add milk, cream, 1 teaspoon essence, remaining 1/2 teaspoon salt and remaining 1/8 teaspoon pepper; whisk to combine. Add the croissants and let sit for 5 minutes. Add the cooked Canadian bacon and sausage, onion mixture and cheese; stir to incorporate the ingredients. Pour into prepared dish, cover with aluminum foil, and bake until almost completely set, about 55 minutes.

Uncover pudding and sprinkle bread crumb mixture evenly over top. Return to oven, increase heat to 375° and bake until pudding is completely set in the center, puffed and golden brown on top, about 20 minutes. Let set for 15 minutes before serving.

Manor on the Creek Bed & Breakfast

2215 East Second Street
Duluth, MN 55812
(218)728-3189
(800)428-3189
www.manoronthecreek.com
manor@manoronthecreek.com

Hosts: Helene & Ernie Agne

*C*harles Duncan was not a Minnesota native, but when he arrived in Duluth in 1881 as a newlywed, he knew he was here to stay. In 1904, after running a successful lumber business and electric company, he built a magnificent yellow brick home with a combination of Neoclassical and Arts and Crafts style architecture. Today, guests are welcomed into Charles' home where examples of original woodwork, such as mahogany and oak fireplace mantles, are found. Guests may choose from 8 spacious suites or rooms, each with a private bath and most with fireplace or whirlpool. Guests may also choose a game of billiards or stroll through our gardens and woods around the Oregon Creek, which adorn our nearly 3 acres of property. A candlelight breakfast is held each day in the oval dining room which overlooks the gardens and creek.

Come and visit the city on the big lake and stay where a common lumberman turned entrepreneur made his home.

Rates at Manor on the Creek Bed & Breakfast range from $125 to $250.
Rates include a full breakfast.

Banana Walnut (Vegan) Pancakes

There are times when I find out about dietary restrictions and realize that there are very few recipes that will suffice. Still, I want breakfast to be as enjoyable for everyone as the bed because, literally, that is the other half of the Bed & Breakfast experience. The first time we tried this recipe to accommodate a vegan guest, we served it to everyone and guess what? The non-vegan guests didn't know they were vegan pancakes! Everyone, including the vegan, thought they were great! Maybe it wouldn't be so bad to be vegan...at least for one meal. I serve them with real maple syrup and a side of fresh fruit for vegans, and, yes, sausage links for the meat lovers. This has become a Manor on the Creek signature item.

Makes 8-10 small pancakes, serving 2-3 pancakes per guest

1-1/2 cups soymilk
1-1/2 teaspoons cider vinegar
    or lemon juice
   3/4 teaspoon baking soda
    1 Tablespoon canola oil
    1 teaspoon vanilla
    3 small to medium bananas,
      mashed with a fork
1-1/2 cups flour
1-1/2 teaspoons baking powder
   1/4 teaspoon salt
   1/8 teaspoon cinnamon
   1/2 cup chopped walnuts

griddle or large nonstick skillet
2 medium mixing bowls
  large wire whip
  medium or large scraper
  large spoon or 1/4 measuring cup
    for dispensing pancake batter

In a medium mixing bowl, mix soymilk cider vinegar. Let stand 5 minutes. In another medium mixing bowl, mix flour, baking powder, salt and cinnamon with wire whip.

Add baking soda, canola oil and vanilla to liquid mixture. Lightly but thoroughly blend with wire whip. Do not over mix. Add bananas to this mixture, lightly blending with scraper. Do not over mix.

Combine liquid mixture with dry mixture, lightly blending with wire whip or scraper. Do not over mix. Fold in nuts with scraper. Do not over mix. If batter is too thick, thin with 1-2 Tablespoons soymilk. Repeat as necessary.

Preheat cooking surface to 350°. When surface is hot, lightly coat cooking surface with canola oil. Ladle pancake batter, about 1/4 cup, on to griddle. Cook 1-1/2 to 2 minutes per side or until side is a medium golden brown, flipping pancakes only once.

Place pancakes on large plate, loosely cover with aluminum foil and place in warming oven. For best results, serve directly from griddle.

With each new batch, lightly re-coat cooking surface with canola oil.

Serve with fruit garnish and a side of real maple syrup. Enjoy!

Another great recipe from Manor on the Creek Bed & Breakfast:

Zucchini-Carrot-Apple Bread

Seasons come and go, and so it goes with zucchini. But when the summer squash comes into season, here is what we do at the Manor.

Makes 10-12 servings

2 cups all-purpose flour	5 mini loaf pans
2 teaspoons ground cinnamon	1 large mixing bowl
1/2 teaspoon ground ginger	1 medium mixing bowl
1/2 teaspoon ground nutmeg	3 small mixing bowls
1/2 teaspoon salt	grater
2 teaspoons baking soda	nut chopper or chopping knife
1-1/4 cups granulated sugar	medium or large scrapers or
3/4 cup canola oil or vegetable oil	large spoon
3 large eggs	measuring spoons and cups
2 teaspoons vanilla extract	wire cooling rack
1-1/2 cups grated zucchini, with skin on	
1-1/2 cups grated carrots	Baking Time: 25-30 minutes
1 small apple, peeled and finely chopped	Baking Temperature: 350°
1/2 cup chopped pecans or walnuts, optional	

Preheat oven to 350°. Coat loaf pans with shortening and flour. In a medium mixing bowl, combine flour, cinnamon, ginger, nutmeg, salt, baking soda and nuts. Lightly mix to ensure even distribution of dry ingredients.

Grate zucchini and carrots into a small mixing bowl. Peel and chop apple.

In a large mixing bowl, combine sugar, oil, eggs and vanilla extract. Stir mixture just until combined; do not over mix. Fold in zucchini, carrots and apple. Fold in dry ingredient mixture just until combined; do not over mix.

Pour batter evenly into the 5 loaf pans. Bake 25-30 minutes, checking regularly to confirm loaves are done. Place on cooling rack for 10 minutes, then remove from pans.

Slice one loaf per couple and serve slightly warm. Enjoy!

Helene's Tiramisu

This is a dessert that we've used for family gatherings and for special occasions with a large group here at the Manor. This great tasting recipe is not overly time-consuming, but it looks like it came right off of the fanciest dessert tray from the best restaurant in town!

Makes 12 generous portions

2 cups espresso coffee or strongly brewed coffee	13" x 9" glass pan
6 pasteurized eggs, separated	2 medium mixing bowls
1/2 cup sugar	large wire whip
3/4 cup Marsala wine	electric mixer
(Marsala wine is a fortified sweet wine produced in Soleras, ideal for baking or cooking)	medium or large scraper
	measuring spoons and cups
1 pound Mascarpone cheese	coffee maker
8 ounces cream cheese	
5 Tablespoons sour cream	
1/2 cup whipping cream	
40 crisp ladyfingers	
unsweetened cocoa	

Brew espresso or strongly brewed coffee and cool thoroughly. (To make strongly brewed coffee, use 4 scoops of 1/3 cup measurement of ground coffee and 2-1/2 cups water, then brew). Separate egg yolks and whites. After separating eggs, discard one egg white.

In a medium mixing bowl, combine sugar with egg yolks. Mix until bright yellow. Mix in Marsala wine.

In another medium mixing bowl, whip Mascarpone cheese, then add cream cheese, sour cream and whipping cream. Whip again.

Combine cheese mixture with yellow egg mixture and beat with mixer at high power for at least 4 minutes. Mixture should be pale yellow.

Whip egg whites in a separate bowl until soft peaks form. Gently fold whipped egg whites into pale yellow mixture.

Layer about 20 ladyfingers in bottom of glass pan. Spoon approximately 2 Tablespoons coffee on each ladyfinger. Cover with cheese mixture. Sprinkle with unsweetened cocoa.

Repeat layers: ladyfingers, coffee, cheese mixture and cocoa. Cover and refrigerate overnight.

To serve, cut into 12 generous servings, place on plates and garnish. Enjoy!

Mathew S. Burrows
1890 Inn Bed & Breakfast

1632 East First Street
Duluth, MN 55812
(218)724-4991
(800)789-1890
www.1890inn.com

Hosts: Alan & Kathy Fink

The Mathew S. Burrows 1890 Inn was built in 1891 for Mathew Burrows, a Duluth clothing retailer. Located only 2-1/2 blocks from Lake Superior on the historic east side of Duluth, the Inn is within walking distance of many restaurants and attractions. The restored Victorian home has two guest rooms and three suites, all with private baths and two have fireplaces. All rooms are furnished with queen-size beds topped with old-fashioned featherbeds and down comforters. Common areas feature fireplaces, a player piano, hand-carved woodwork, cathedral glass windows, and comfortable porches—front and back. A full breakfast and evening snacks are provided.

Rates at Mathew S. Burrows 1890 Inn Bed & Breakfast range from $95 to $185.
Rates include a full breakfast.

Austrian Apple Pancakes

This dish is always a hit! Serve it with sour cream, and your guests will rave.

Serves 4

6 **Granny Smith apples, peeled,**
   cored, and sliced
2 **Tablespoons butter**
1 **cup sugar**
2 **Tablespoons cornstarch**
1 **teaspoon cinnamon**
4 **Tablespoons water or apple juice**
6 **eggs**
6 **Tablespoons flour**
6 **Tablespoons milk**
   Pinch of sugar and salt

   10" cast iron fry pan or 4 5"soufflé dishes
   Two small mixing bowls

   Baking Time: 20 minutes
   Baking Temperature: 400°

Preheat oven to 400°. Spray fry pan with nonstick cooking spray and melt butter. Add apples, sugar, cinnamon, cornstarch and water. Stir to dissolve sugar and moisten apples. Set mixture aside.

Separate eggs; whites in one bowl and yolks in the other. Add flour, milk, sugar and salt to yolks. Blend until mixture becomes light.

Beat egg whites until stiff peaks form. Fold into yolk mixture and spoon over apples in fry pan. (Apples may be transferred to 4 soufflé dishes for baking.) Bake for 20 minutes.

Invert pancake on platter for serving. Serve with sour cream on the side.

French Puffs

This is an easy, tasty recipe! We usually make a double recipe...just double the ingredients.

Makes 12 muffins

1-1/2 **cups all-purpose flour**
   2 **teaspoons baking powder**
1-1/2 **cups sugar**
   1/2 **teaspoon salt**
   1/2 **teaspoon nutmeg**
   2/3 **cup buttermilk**
      1 **egg**
   1/2 **cup melted butter**

Topping:
   1/2 **cup sugar**
   1/2 **teaspoon cinnamon**
   1/4 **cup melted butter**
While muffins are baking, mix sugar and cinnamon in a shallow bowl. Melt butter.

   2 **medium mixing bowls**
      muffin tin

      Baking Time: 20-25 minutes
      Baking Temperature: 350°

Preheat oven to 350°. In a medium mixing bowl, combine flour, sugar, salt, baking powder and nutmeg. Make a well in the center of dry mixture.

In another medium mixing bowl, lightly beat egg. Add buttermilk and melted butter. Place wet mixture in well of dry mixture; combine only until moistened. Do not over mix.

Fill muffin cups 2/3 full and bake for 20-25 minutes. Tops should be golden brown.

When baked muffins are cool enough to handle, dip tops in melted butter and then in cinnamon/sugar mixture.

Tips for Making the Best Muffins

These great helpful hints for baking muffins will save you time and make your baking experience a pleasure!

1. For those times when you only need one or two muffins and find it difficult to adjust the measurements for a small batch, make a full batch and freeze the unused portion.

   After batter is mixed, take the extra batter and spoon it into paper muffin cups that have been placed in an extra muffin tin. Place the extra tin in the freezer. The next day, remove frozen muffins and place in a freezer bag.

   Take muffins out of freezer and place in muffin tin 1/2 hour before baking. Bake muffins as directed; you may need to add several minutes to the baking time.

2. To make boxed muffin mix taste more like made-from-scratch, add 2 heaping Tablespoons of Bisquick® to dry mix.

3. Substitute buttermilk for milk or water in muffin recipes for moister and richer tasting muffins.

4. You can use frozen fruit in muffin recipes; add several minutes to the baking time.

5. Baked muffins are best stored at room temperature for use the next day.

6. Don't let muffins cool completely in muffin tins as they may develop a metallic taste. Remove muffins from tin while still warm and allow to cool on a glass plate.

7. Don't wash muffin tins in the dishwasher because the tins will rust. A light coating of oil after hand washing helps to keep tins rust-free.

Olcott House
Bed & Breakfast

2316 East 1st Street
Duluth, MN 55812
(218)728-1339
(800)715-1339
www.olcotthouse.com
info@olcotthouse.com

Hosts: Barb & Don Trueman

The Olcott House is a *Gone With the Wind* 1904 historic Georgian Colonial mansion featuring six recently refurbished guest rooms/suites. Located in the quiet historic residential mansion district of Duluth, the house is just four blocks from the shore of Lake Superior and the beautiful Lakewalk, minutes to attractions, shopping and incredible North Shore scenery. Guest areas include a grand porch, library, music room, parlor, two dining rooms, arbor/fountain garden area and a gift shop in the old ballroom, featuring Minnesota artists and craftspeople. All rooms have private baths and most have working fireplaces, private porches or decks, period antiques and are smoke-free. Every evening, refreshments are provided, and every morning, a sumptuous breakfast awaits you. Barb and Don Trueman, owners, welcome you to their historic home!

Rates at Olcott House Bed & Breakfast range from $125 to $225.
Rates include a full breakfast.

Blueberry Vanilla Yogurt Muffins

The Olcott House serves these muffins with egg specialties and everyone always loves them! They are easy to make – we pop them out of the oven 5 minutes before serving.

Makes 12 muffins

Muffins:
2 eggs
1 cup sugar
1 teaspoon vanilla
1 cup vanilla yogurt
2 cups all-purpose flour
1/2 teaspoon baking soda
1 teaspoon baking powder
1 teaspoon cinnamon
1 cup fresh blueberries

1 small mixing bowl
1 medium mixing bowl
mixing spoon
muffin pan for 12 muffins

Baking Time: 17-20 minutes
Baking Temperature: 375°

Topping:
1/2 cup brown sugar
1/2 teaspoon cinnamon
1/2 cup chopped walnuts
Mix ingredients together and spoon on top of muffins before baking.

Preheat oven to 375°. In a small mixing bowl, beat eggs. Add sugar, vanilla, yogurt and mix well. In a medium mixing bowl, combine dry ingredients together. Mix dry ingredients into yogurt mixture just until moistened. Do not over mix. Fold in blueberries. Spoon into greased muffin tins. Sprinkle tops of muffins with topping mixture.

Bake for 17-20 minutes or until muffin tops are a light golden brown.

Crunchy French Toast

A new twist to French Toast that is always a crowd-pleaser. Try a variety of fruit toppings. We have found that adding Amaretto also makes this French Toast special. Try it, you'll like it!

Serves 4

8 slices French bread, sliced diagonally, 1" thick
3 large eggs
2-1/2 cups milk
1 Tablespoon sugar
1 teaspoon vanilla
3 cups corn flakes, crushed
2 Tablespoons Amaretto, optional
butter for griddle
8 fresh sliced strawberries
powdered sugar for dusting

1 large mixing bowl
whisk
griddle
cake pan (to crush corn flakes in)

In a large mixing bowl, beat eggs, milk, sugar, vanilla and Amaretto together until well mixed. Soak bread in egg mix. Press each piece of bread in crushed corn flakes, coating both sides of bread.

Preheat griddle to high (375°-400°). Melt butter, then place bread on griddle. Cook for approximately 3-1/2 minutes on each side or until golden.

Serve immediately while hot and crunchy. Garnish with strawberries and dust with powdered sugar.

Homemade Syrup:
1/2 cup butter
1/2 cup milk
1 teaspoon vanilla
1 cup brown sugar
1 cup of your favorite maple syrup *(I use Mrs. Butterworth)*

In a saucepan, stir all ingredients slowly over low heat. Do not boil. Serve when hot and mixed.

Scrambled Eggs with Spinach

This dish goes well with grilled smoked ham and your favorite muffins, warmed. Garnish with fresh fruit.

Makes 6 servings

        12 eggs
       1/2 cup water
         1 bag (10 ounces) frozen spinach, thawed,
               drained and patted dry
         1 small onion, minced
       1/2 cup shredded Swiss cheese
         1 teaspoon garlic and herb seasoning
         1 package (1.25 ounces) Hollandaise sauce
               (prepared according to package instructions)
            butter to taste
            olive oil

         1 large mixing bowl
            large skillet

In a large mixing bowl, beat eggs and water together. Cover bottom of hot skillet sparingly with olive oil. Add minced onions and cook slightly. Add egg mixture.

Once eggs are almost scrambled, add spinach and garlic/herb seasoning; mix well. Add a couple of pats of butter for a rich taste. When scrambled eggs are done, mix in cheese.

Serve while hot and top with prepared Hollandaise sauce. Another version of this dish is to serve the scrambled eggs on top of pastry shells that have been prepared in advance and are still hot.

Solglimt on the Water

828 Lake Avenue South
Duluth, MN 55802
(218)727-0596
(877)727-0596
www.solglimt.com
grovers@solglimt.com

Hosts: Brian & Mary Grover

*W*hen water, sun and wind unite, they create an illusion of glittering sparkles on the waves-christened Solglimt in Denmark…dancing diamond. Discover a similar array of extraordinary, unexpected delights at Duluth's Solglimt Bed & Breakfast, located on the sandy shores of Lake Superior. A place where peace and the serenity of the sun reach down to touch the shore, Solglimt Bed & Breakfast…

Rates at Solglimt on the Water range from $125 to $205.
Rates include a full breakfast.

Poached Eggs with Roasted Tomatoes & Portobellos

This delicious egg recipe is elegant yet simple.

Serves 4

4   Portobello mushroom caps, stems discarded
2   plum tomatoes, halved lengthwise
3   Tablespoons olive oil
1   teaspoon white vinegar
4   eggs
1/2 teaspoon balsamic vinegar
1/4 cup Fontina cheese, grated
1   Tablespoon finely chopped chives
    salt and pepper

10" skillet for poaching eggs
broiler pan or vegetable rack for gas grill

Preheat the broiler or gas grill. Brush the mushrooms and tomatoes with olive oil and sprinkle with salt and pepper. Arrange mushrooms, stemmed side down, and tomato halves, cut side up, in broiler pan or vegetable rack. Broil the vegetables 6" from heat, turning the mushrooms over halfway through cooking, until tender and tomatoes are slightly charred.

While vegetables are cooking, fill a skillet with 2 inches of water. Add white vinegar and bring to a simmer. Break the eggs into a cup and slide gently into the water. Poach for about 4 minutes or until whites are set. Remove with a slotted spoon and dab with paper towel to dry.

Sprinkle stemmed side of mushrooms with balsamic vinegar, then put one tomato half on mushroom and top with egg. Cover egg with grated cheese and return to heat until cheese is melted. Sprinkle with chives.

Recipe Note:
We very finely chop colored peppers, sauté them in butter and sprinkle them all over the plate for added color.

Blue Heron
Bed & Breakfast

827 Kawishiwi Trail
Ely, MN 55731
(218)365-4720
www.blueheronbnb.com
info@blueheronbnb.com

Hosts: Jo Kovach, Pat & Josie Milan

Blue Heron Bed & Breakfast is a lakeside lodge on land adjoining the Boundary Waters Canoe Area Wilderness (BWCAW). At the Blue Heron, you can experience all the wilderness of a canoe trip and return to a king size bed, private bath and meals in the dining room overlooking the lake. By boat or on foot, you can explore the nooks and crannies of our 10 acres and the millions of acres of BWCAW, which is right next door. Numerous trails and logging roads are nearby for hiking, biking and skiing. Or perhaps you would rather "just be" – dangle your feet off the deck or relax on the deck. In the evening, we frequently enjoy friendly campfires and awesome shows, courtesy of the Northern Lights.

Blue Heron is a haven of quiet simplicity, where you can experience a connection with wilderness and water. Come, be as active, or as idle, as you wish.

Rates at Blue Heron Bed & Breakfast range from $110 to $175.
Rates include a full breakfast.

Gingerbread Pancakes

Mmm.....the fresh scent of gingerbread in the morning! Serve with real maple syrup, chopped pecans and whipped cream for a mouth-watering experience!

Serves 4

1-1/4	cups all-purpose flour
1	cup whole wheat flour
2	Tablespoons brown sugar
1-1/2	teaspoons baking powder
1-1/2	teaspoons baking soda
1	teaspoon ground cinnamon
1	teaspoon ground nutmeg
1	teaspoon ground ginger
1/2	teaspoon ground cloves
1/2	teaspoon salt
2	cups buttermilk
1/4	cup molasses
2	eggs
1	small mixing bowl
1	large mixing bowl or
	wide-mouth pitcher
	nonstick griddle
	whisk
	spatula

In a wide-mouth pitcher or large mixing bowl, combine all-purpose flour, whole wheat flour, brown sugar, baking powder, baking soda, cinnamon, nutmeg, ginger, cloves and salt.

In a small mixing bowl, whisk together buttermilk, molasses and eggs. Stir into flour mixture just until moistened.

Coat a nonstick griddle or large skillet with nonstick cooking spray and heat to medium heat. For each pancake, pour a ladle, about 1/4 cup batter, on to the griddle. Cook for 1-2 minutes or until pancakes are bubbly and slightly dry around the edges. Turn over and cook briefly until golden.

Serve immediately with chopped pecans, whipped cream and maple syrup.

Akin House
Bed & Breakfast

19185 Akin Road
Farmington, MN 55024
(651)463-1298
www.akinhouse.com
akinhouse@charter.com

Hosts: Bruce & Sharon Conner

The Akin House Bed & Breakfast is located in Farmington, a southern suburb of Minneapolis/St. Paul. The house, built in 1854, exhibits many characteristics historically associated with the Italian Villa (also called Italianate) style. More than 150 years ago, Mrs. Akin brought with her, from New York, a slip of Virginia Creeper, which to this day graces the exterior walls of the home. The Akin House was placed on the National Register of Historic Places in 1979 and is also recognized by the Farmington Heritage Landmark Commission. The Vermillion River, just three miles south of the Akin House Bed & Breakfast, boasts some of the state's best trout fishing. There are five golf courses within 20 minutes; there are many miles of community walking and biking trails; and tennis courts are only a block away. Other local activities include the Mall of America, Minnesota Zoo, Mystic Lake Casino and the Twin Cities International Airport. Our guest rooms and common areas have been lovingly restored to that quiet elegance of years past, yet with today's modern touches, including whirlpool suites, stereos in each room and TV/VCR/DVD access. We offer a smoke-free environment and children and pets are welcome by arrangement.

Rates at Akin House Bed & Breakfast range from $100 to $120.
Rates include a full breakfast.

Cherry-Oatmeal Cookies

Guests arriving at the Akin House Bed & Breakfast in Farmington are sure to be greeted with a plate of freshly baked Cherry-Oatmeal Cookies and a glass of ice-cold lemonade. Sharon Conner keeps a stack of this recipe on hand as guests always ask for the trade secret!

Makes 4 dozen cookies

1-1/2	**cups all-purpose flour**
1	**teaspoon ground cinnamon**
1/2	**teaspoon salt**
1/2	**teaspoon baking soda**
1/2	**teaspoon baking powder**
1	**cup (2 sticks) butter**
1	**cup dark brown sugar**
1/2	**cup white granulated sugar**
2	**large eggs**
1	**teaspoon pure vanilla extract**
2	**cups old-fashioned rolled oats** *(do not use quick oats)*
2	**cups dried sour cherries** *(check the bulk section at your local grocer or natural foods store. May be listed as "sweetened dried cherries")*
1	**medium mixing bowl**
1	**large mixing bowl**
	baking sheet or baking stone
	parchment paper
	electric mixer

Baking Time: 20 minutes
Baking Temperature: 350°

Preheat oven to 350°. Line baking sheet with parchment paper (not necessary if using a baking stone). In a medium mixing bowl, whisk flour, cinnamon, salt, soda and powder. Set aside.

Using an electric mixer with paddle attachment or a hand mixer, beat butter and both sugars until light and fluffy, about 1-2 minutes. Add eggs and vanilla and beat long enough to fully incorporate ingredients. Add dry ingredients to butter mixture, beating on low speed to combine. Stir in oats and cherries.

Using a 2-ounce scoop, place on baking sheet, leaving 6" between cookies. Bake for 20 minutes or until edges are just turning brown. Cool 2 minutes before transferring cookies to a cooling rack.

Bakketopp Hus
Bed & Breakfast

20571 Hillcrest Road
Fergus Falls, MN 56537
(218)739-2915
(800)739-2915
www.bbonline.com/MN/Bakketopp
DDN@prtel.com

Hosts: Dennis and Judy Nims

What the experts are saying about Bakketopp Hus:
Quotes from our guests:

"Where the challenges of everyday life can be shut out for a time. Where time stands still to allow us to rediscover our love. Where there is nothing that intrudes but peace. Thank you for making it possible."

"These last two nights in your home were absolutely fabulous! Wonderful food, warm hospitality – a time to remember."

"It was so nice to be spoiled for a day."

"We loved it here from the moment of our arrival. It's simply perfect. You made it memorable. We'll be back."

"What a lovely respite from the hustle and bustle of the city. This was a perfect setting for my dearest friend and me to meet, talk, laugh and remind ourselves how God has blessed us."

THIS IS BAKKETOPP

Rates at Bakketopp Hus Bed & Breakfast range from $85 to $120.
Rates include a full breakfast.

Orange Chipper Scones

Scones are always a great addition to any breakfast or brunch. This recipe is easy to make and delicious to eat!

Makes 24 scones

4 cups all-purpose flour
4 teaspoons baking powder
1 cup granulated sugar
1/2 teaspoon baking soda
1/2 teaspoon salt
1 cup semi-sweet small chocolate chips
1 Tablespoons grated orange peel
2 sticks (1 cup) unsalted butter, cut and softened
1 cup buttermilk
3 large eggs
1 teaspoon orange extract
1 Tablespoon milk
1 cup golden raisins

Icing:
2 cups powdered sugar
1/4 cup orange juice
1 Tablespoon grated orange peel
1 teaspoon orange extract
Combine all ingredients in a medium mixing bowl. Mix until smooth.

2 small mixing bowls
1 medium mixing bowl
1 large mixing bowl
2 baking sheets

Baking Time: 18-22 minutes
Baking Temperature: 350°

Preheat oven to 350°. Grease baking sheets. In a large mixing bowl, combine flour, granulated sugar, baking powder, baking soda and salt. Add chips, raisins and orange peel; mix well. Cut in butter with a pastry blender or two knives until mixture resembles coarse crumbs. In a small mixing bowl, combine buttermilk, two eggs, and orange extract. Pour buttermilk mixture into flour mixture; mix just until sticky dough is formed. Do not over mix. Drop by 1/4 cupfuls onto prepared baking sheets.

In a small mixing bowl, combine remaining egg and milk. Brush egg mixture over top of dough. Sprinkle tops with sugar.

Bake for 18-22 minutes or until wooden toothpick inserted in center comes out clean. Bake one sheet at a time. Cool on wire racks for 10 minutes. Drizzle scones with icing (above) and serve warm. Toasted almonds or pecan pieces are also an optional topping.

Another great recipe from Bakketopp Hus Bed & Breakfast:

Strawberry Dessert

This is a wonderfully easy dessert that will impress your guests and delight your taste buds! You will need to be sure to prepare this ahead of time.

Makes 12 servings

1/2 teaspoon cream of tartar
1/4 teaspoon salt
1-1/3 cups sugar
1 cup sugar
1 teaspoon vanilla
2 packages (8 ounces each)
    cream cheese
1 pint whipping cream
2 cups miniature
    marshmallows

Topping:
1 can (21 ounces) cherry
    pie filling
1/4 teaspoon cinnamon
1 teaspoon lemon juice
1 box (10 ounces) frozen
    strawberries, thawed,
    or fresh

In a medium mixing bowl, combine all ingredients. Top dessert just before serving.

1 small mixing bowl
2 medium mixing bowls
2 large mixing bowls
9" x 13" pan

Baking Time: 60 minutes
Baking Temperature: 275°

Preheat oven to 275°. In a large mixing bowl, beat egg whites with cream of tartar and salt. Gradually add sugar, beating until stiff. Pour into greased pan and bake for 60 minutes. Turn off oven and leave pan in oven over night.

The next morning, in a medium mixing bowl, beat sugar, vanilla and cream cheese until creamy. In a small mixing bowl, beat whipping cream. Fold into cream cheese mixture. Add miniature marshmallows. Spread over meringue and refrigerate over night.

When ready to serve, spread topping over cream cheese mixture.

Another great recipe from Bakketopp Hus Bed & Breakfast:

Banana Split Dessert

This is a great dessert for those ice cream lovers in your life!

Makes 12 servings

Crust:
1-1/2 boxes (16 ounces each)
graham crackers, crushed
1/3 cup melted butter

Filling:
1/4 cup butter
1 cup powdered sugar
3/4 cup evaporated milk
1 teaspoon vanilla
3-5 bananas, sliced
1/2 gallon vanilla ice cream, sliced
into 1/2" pieces
3/4 pint whipped cream
nuts, optional
chocolate topping, optional

2 medium mixing bowls
saucepan
9" x 13" pan

Baking Time: 8 minutes
Baking Temperature: 350°

Preheat oven to 350°. In a medium mixing bowl, combine graham cracker crumbs and butter until moist. Spread in bottom of pan, reserving 1/4 cup for topping. Bake for 8 minutes.

In saucepan, cook butter, powdered sugar and evaporated milk until mixture is thick and smooth, stirring constantly. Add vanilla. Cool or chill in refrigerator.

Place sliced bananas evenly over crust. Place ice cream slices over bananas. Cover ice cream with nuts, if desired. Spread cooled powdered sugar mixture over nuts. Top with whipped cream. Sprinkle reserved graham crackers over top and freeze.

May be served with chocolate topping or flavor of your choice.

Poplar Creek Guesthouse Bed & Breakfast

11 Poplar Creek Drive
Grand Marais, MN 55604
(218)388-4487
(800)322-8327
www.poplarcreekbb.com
bct@boundarycountry.com

Hosts: Barbara & Ted Young

Poplar Creek Guesthouse Bed & Breakfast is a secluded, peaceful mid-Gunflint Trail inn and lake cabin. The Inn overlooks the Boundary Waters Canoe Area (BWCA), canoe-only Little Ollie Lake and Creek. We are 30 miles inland from Lake Superior. All breakfasts include fruit plate, two juices, meats, entrée, dessert and organic fresh ground coffee and hot water.

Poplar Creek Guesthouse has two B & B rooms and two room suites. One room has a double whirlpool tub and queen-size bed. The other room has a double shower and two queen-size beds. Guests enjoy a common kitchen, dining/lounge area with fireplace and deck with a great view of the creek and lake. Suites include a bedroom with queen-size bed and a second room with compact kitchen, dining/living room area, fireplace and private deck. All rooms have private, shower bathrooms and in-room data port phones. There is a main floor common area and sun porch. Our Inn is smoke-free and no pets, please.

Packages include: honeymoons/anniversaries; special times for two; inn to inn hiking, mountain biking and canoeing; Mongolian firepot dinner; dog sledding/B & B stay; sleigh ride; and on the Beargrease Trail. Gift certificates are available.

Summer activities include hiking, mountain biking, canoeing, fishing and swimming. There are many restaurants and gift shops nearby, and we are adjacent to Lima Mountain Road Birding Area. Guided day canoe trips are available to beautiful Rose Lake and include lunch. Begin and end your BWCA canoe trip at our B&B. Winter activities on the premises include cross-country skiing and snowshoeing. Lodge to lodge and yurt to yurt ski treks are available.

Rates at Poplar Creek Guesthouse Bed & Breakfast range from $99 to $135.
Rates include a full breakfast.

Stuffed French Toast

Breakfast starts with an artfully arranged fresh fruit plate, followed by the breakfast entrée. Among the entrees served are: Stuffed French Toast, egg casserole, Finnish pancakes or waffles. A side dish of bacon, pork sausage, Swedish potato sausage or ham is served with the entrée. Finally, no breakfast is complete without a dessert! Various desserts are served at the end of the meal, including maple-baked stuffed pears, glazed-fried peaches, fried bananas and baked apples. The dessert is surrounded by whipped cream and topped with flaked coconut, crystallized ginger, fresh fruit or grated dark chocolate.

Serves 4

1 **loaf day old French bread, about 5" across**
   (fresh bread is too soft to slice)
8 **ounces Ricotta cheese**
   (may be regular, low fat or no fat)
8 **ounces cream cheese**
   (may be regular, low fat or no fat)
1/4 **cup apricot preserves**
1/4 **cups ground pecans**
1/4 **teaspoon maple flavoring**
1/4 **teaspoon rum flavoring**
6 **eggs** *(I use 3 eggs for 2 people)*
2/3 **cup milk** *(I use 1/6 cup milk for each person)*

mixer
1 **medium mixing bowl**
1 **shallow bowl**
   griddle

Put the Ricotta and cream cheese in a mixer and beat until mixed together. Add the preserves, then the nuts and, lastly, the flavorings. Beat. Set aside or refrigerate in covered container.

Slice off ends of bread at a diagonal to expose more bread. Slice the rest of the bread 1-1/2" wide at diagonal. I use two slices of bread per person. When all the bread is sliced, take a smaller knife and make a slit in the middle of each slice, being careful not to cut to the bottom or too far down the sides. You want to make a pocket. Make pockets in all the slices you need.

Scoop about 1 Tablespoon or more of the cheese mixture and dollop into the bread pocket. Be careful not to let too much drip out.

In a shallow bowl, make a dipping mixture of the eggs and milk. Sometimes I use less milk, and sometimes I've used evaporated milk to make a richer mixture. Beat the mixture.

Get a griddle ready. Spray the griddle with nonstick cooking spray. Do not burn the spray. Dip the stuffed bread into the egg/milk mixture. Let extra mixture drip off the bread, then set on griddle and fry each side until golden. The pieces will fry quickly.

We serve the French Toast with maple syrup harvested right here in Cook County.

Maple Baked Stuffed Pears

This wonderful recipe is fabulous for breakfast, brunch or any time of day! Serve with real whipping and sliced strawberries.

Serves 4

4	**pears, firm and ripe** *(I prefer nicely shaped pears, such as Anjou or small Bartlett)*
1/4	**cup craisins**
3	**Tablespoons chopped walnuts**
2-1/2	**Tablespoons sugar**
1	**Tablespoon lemon juice**
1/4	**cup water**
1/4	**cup maple syrup**
1	**medium mixing bowl**
1	**deep baking dish with lid**

Baking Time: 1 hour
Baking Temperature: 350°

Preheat oven to 350°. Peel the pears, leaving the stems on. Core the bottom ends and slice a thin piece off the bottom so pears stand upright.

To make the filling, combine craisins, walnuts, sugar and lemon juice in a medium mixing bowl; mix well.

Fill the cavity of each pear with an equal amount of filling. Stand pears upright in baking dish and pour water in dish. Pour maple syrup over pears. Cover the dish with lid or domed aluminum foil.

Bake for about 1 hour or until pears are easily pierced with a fork. After 1/2 hour of baking, I like to take the dish out of the oven and spoon the hot maple syrup and water over the pears. Then return the pears to the oven. After the pears are baked, spoon the sauce over the pears as they cool.

To serve, real whipping cream is spooned in front of the pear and sliced strawberries are set upright on one end of the whipped cream. Then whipped cream is spooned on top and mint leaves are set in the whipped cream.

Sautéed Peaches

I like serving a warm breakfast dessert. It is such a surprise to my guests! If guests are staying a few days, they like to guess what the breakfast dessert will be. These are great when served with whipped cream and sliced strawberries or whole raspberries.

Serves 4

4 ripe peaches
2 Tablespoons unsalted butter
1 teaspoon rum flavoring
1/4 cup maple syrup

saucepan
slotted spoon
large fry pan

Drop the peaches into boiling water for a few seconds. Remove the peaches with a slotted spoon. Rinse the peaches under cold water. Slice each peach in half, peel off the skin and remove the pits.

Cut each peach half into quarters. You will end up with 8 slices for each dessert plate.

On medium heat, melt the butter in a large pan that can hold all cut peach slices. Add rum flavoring to melted butter and stir. Add peach slices, cut side down. Spoon maple syrup over peach slices. Heat for 10-15 minutes. Turn heat down, if necessary. Turn over peach slices. Spoon the butter and maple syrup over peach slices. Keep heating on medium heat until peach slices are cooked through, another 15 minutes.

Carefully arrange 8 peach slices for each person on a dessert plate in a pretty pattern. After peach slices have cooled, spoon whipped cream in the center of the plate. Add sliced strawberries or whole raspberries to the whipped cream and serve.

Morning Glory
Bed & Breakfast

726 NW Second Avenue
Grand Rapids, MN 55744
(218)326-3978
(866)926-3978
www.morningglorybandb.com
morningglory@grandrapids-mn.com

Hosts: Karen & Ron Herbig

Anytime of year is great in beautiful northern Minnesota and the Morning Glory is at the center of it all! Enjoy scenic byways, biking, lakes, skiing, shopping and much more while letting the Morning Glory surround you in casually elegant comfort with four spacious suites and private baths. Two suites have gas fireplaces and one a whirlpool. Sit by the fire in the livingroom in winter or stroll the gardens,sip a cool drink under the pergola in summer. Guests enjoy a full breakfast weekdays and on weekends are treated to a sumptuous 3-course breakfast and wine/cheese social time in the early evening. The Morning Glory pampers the honeymooners, traveler and business person alike!

Rates at Morning Glory Bed & Breakfast range from $85 to $120.
Rates include a full breakfast.

Ham & Cheese Florentine

This is a great nontraditional breakfast – only 1 egg! All of our guests love it, and it's very quick to make!

Serves 4-6

1/2 package (16 ounce package) frozen
　　　puff pastry (1 sheet)
　2 green onions, chopped
　2 Tablespoons chopped pimento
1/2 teaspoon oregano leaves, crushed
1/2 pound smoked ham slices
1/2 pound turkey slices
　1 cup spinach leaves
　4 ounces shredded or sliced Swiss cheese
　1 egg
　1 Tablespoon water

　2 small mixing bowls
　　lightly floured board
　　jelly roll pan or baking sheet

　　Baking Time: 25 minutes
　　Baking Temperature: 400°

Thaw pastry at room temperature for 30 minutes. Preheat oven to 400°. In a small mixing bowl, mix onions, pimento and oregano. Unfold pastry on lightly floured board and roll into 16" x 12" rectangle. With long side facing you, layer ham, turkey, spinach and cheese on bottom half, within 1" of edges. Sprinkle with onion mixture, and starting with filled side, roll like jelly roll. Place on baking sheet seam-side down and tuck under ends.

In a small mixing bowl, combine egg and water. Brush roll with egg mixture. Bake for 25 minutes.

Classic Rosewood
– A Thorwood Property

620 Ramsey Street
Hastings, MN 55033
(651)437-3297
(888)846-7966
www.thorwoodinn.com
info@thorwoodinn.com

Hosts: Dick & Pam Thorsen

A warm welcome awaits you at Classic Rosewood, a 1880 National Register Queen Anne. Dick and Pam Thorsen have been welcoming guests since 1983 at Rosewood's sister Inn, the Thorwood. Thorsen's rescued this condemned property in 1987 and opened after an extensive, award-winning restoration in 1989.

Choose from a comfy rocker, a porch swing or a loveseat focused on a glowing fireplace. Offerings include in-suite massage, in-house intimate dinners and a help-yourself pantry. Guests always choose breakfast time and place. Seven of the eight suites have a double whirlpool and fireplace.

Nearby are ten golf courses, two ski resorts and a bike path that is almost all waterway. Don't miss Carpenter Nature Center, the Alexis Bailly Vineyard and Winery, the gothic revival LeDuc Mansion and the Vermillion Falls.

Rates at Classic Rosewood – A Thorwood Property range from $97 to $277.
Rates include a full breakfast.

Egg-Potato Florentine

A hearty yet elegant dish. This entrée works well in individual ramekins. It's a favorite as the spinach and fresh potatoes are a welcome surprise.

Serves 12

      1 bag (1.25 pounds) fresh shredded potatoes
      1 package (10 ounces) frozen spinach, thawed
           and drained
      2 shallots, finely chopped
      1 can (10.5 ounces) cream of celery soup
      1 cup sour cream
      2 cups shredded Colby Jack cheese, divided
    12 eggs
      4 cups half-and-half
      1 cup chopped ham, optional
      1 medium mixing bowl
      1 large mixing bowl
    12 ramekins

      Baking Time: 35-45 minutes
      Baking Temperature: 350º

   Preheat oven to 350º. In a large mixing bowl, combine first 6 ingredients (potatoes through 1 cup cheese). In a medium mixing bowl, mix eggs and half-and-half. Do not beat.

   Spoon potato mixture into sprayed ramekins, approximately 3 heaping Tablespoons each. Add egg mixture, filling ramekins to about 1" from top. Sprinkle with remaining cheese. Bake for 35-45 minutes.

Herb-Crusted Salmon with Sun-Dried Tomato Sauce

Salmon lovers will delight in this great recipe! This is an elegant entrée that will be sure to impress your guests!

Serves 4

1 Tablespoon fresh basil, minced, or 1 teaspoon crumbled dried basil

1 Tablespoon fresh thyme, minced, or 1 teaspoon crumbled dried thyme

2 teaspoons fresh rosemary leaves, minced, or 1/2 teaspoon crumbled dried rosemary

1/2 cup dry bread crumbs

2 (12 ounces each) skinless salmon fillets

Sun-dried tomato sauce:

4 teaspoons olive oil, divided

2 Tablespoons shallots, minced

1 Tablespoon lemon juice, strained

1/2 cup dry white wine

6 sun-dried tomatoes (not packed in oil), finely minced

1/2 teaspoon coarse salt

1/2 teaspoon fresh ground black pepper

10-inch nonstick skillet

9" x 13" x 2" ovenproof casserole dish

wax paper

Baking Time: 8-10 minutes

Baking Temperature: 400°

Sauce Preparation:

In skillet, heat 2 teaspoons oil over medium heat. Add shallots and sauté, stirring constantly, until lightly golden, about 1 minute. Add lemon juice, wine, and sun-dried tomatoes. Turn heat to medium-high and cook until sauce is reduced to 1/2 cup, about 2 minutes. Season with salt and pepper and set aside. (Sauce can be made up to 1 hour before cooking fish. Reheat over low heat just before removing fish from oven.)

Fillets:

Adjust oven rack to center of oven and preheat oven to 400°. Lightly grease casserole dish with nonstick cooking spray; set aside.

On a piece of wax paper, combine basil, thyme, rosemary and bread crumbs. Dredge each fillet in bread crumb mixture, coating well. Transfer fillets to prepared pan and place 2 inches apart. Drizzle with remaining 2 teaspoons oil.

Bake just until fish is opaque and barely flakes when tested in the center with a knife, about 8-10 minutes. Transfer to serving platter, slice each fillet in half crosswise, spoon sauce over fillets and serve.

Rosie's Vegetarian Chili with Avocado Salsa

This is a very nice chili, but the avocado salsa, sour cream and lime really make it special! Prepare the salsa while the chili simmers. It's best served soon after the ingredients are combined.

Makes 6 bowls or 1 large tureen for a romantic, graze-all-night supper

2   teaspoons canola oil
1   cup chopped onion
1   cup chopped red bell pepper
2   teaspoons chili powder
1   teaspoon ground cumin
1   teaspoon dried oregano
3   garlic cloves, minced
1   can (4.5 ounces) chopped green chilies
2/3 cup uncooked quick-cooking barley *(if you cannot find quick-cooking, use regular; just allow more time for cooking)*
1/4 cup water
1   can (15 ounces) black beans, drained

1   can (14.5 ounces) diced tomatoes, undrained
1   can (14.5 ounces) vegetable broth
3   Tablespoons fresh chopped cilantro
6   Tablespoons sour cream
6   lime wedges
18 baked tortilla chips

    Dutch oven
1   small mixing bowl

Heat oil in Dutch oven over medium-high heat. Add onion and bell pepper; sauté for 3 minutes. Add chili powder, cumin, oregano, garlic and green chilies; cook for 1 minute. Stir in barley, black beans, tomatoes and broth; bring to a boil. Cover, reduce heat and simmer for 20 minutes or until barley is tender. Stir in cilantro.

Spoon chili into soup bowls and top each serving with sour cream, lime wedges, chips and avocado salsa. You may store chili in an airtight container in the refrigerator for up to 2 days.

Avocado Salsa:
1/2 cup finely chopped, peeled avocado
1/3 cup chopped, seeded tomato
2   Tablespoons finely chopped onion
1   Tablespoon finely chopped, seeded jalapeno pepper
1   Tablespoon chopped fresh cilantro
1   Tablespoon fresh lime juice
1/8 teaspoon salt

In a small mixing bowl, combine all ingredients and toss gently. Serve immediately.

Nicolin Mansion
Bed & Breakfast

221 Broadway Street South
Jordan, MN 55352
(952)492-6441
www.nicolinmansion.com
info@nicolinmansion.com

Hosts: Kevin & Terri Knox

The 1888 Nicolin Mansion, a property on the National Register of Historic Places, is located in the downtown Jordan historic district, amid antique shoppes, family restaurants and town parks that lie beside beautiful Sand Creek and Waterfall. Each guest room is unique, inspired by the former mansion owner for which it is named. A full gourmet breakfast, featuring locally cured sausage and locally grown apples, is served by candlelight in our grand dining room.

Rates at Nicolin Mansion Bed & Breakfast range from $100 to $140.
Rates include a full breakfast.

Apple Coffee Kuchen

This recipe has been adapted from a recipe served for years at Jordan's Triangle Café, celebrating the 150-year-old community's German heritage and the local apple orchards. The Nicolin Mansion features this recipe for dessert during September's annual Heimatfest and throughout the fall. If, by chance, there is any left over, it makes a fantastic bread pudding.

Serves 12

2 cups flour	1 small mixing bowl
1 teaspoon baking powder	1 large mixing bowl
1 teaspoon baking soda	sifter
1/2 cup butter, softened	electric mixer
3/4 cup sugar	bundt pan
1 teaspoon vanilla	1-cup glass measure
3 eggs	
1/2 pint sour cream	Baking Time: 1 hour
6 Tablespoons butter, melted	Baking Temperature: 350°
1 cup apples, peeled, cored and chopped	
1 cup packed brown sugar	
2 teaspoons cinnamon	

Preheat oven to 350°. Sift together flour, baking powder, and baking soda. In a large mixing bowl, cream together softened butter, sugar and vanilla until light and fluffy. Add eggs and beat well. Add sifted dry ingredients alternately with sour cream. Add the melted butter and mix thoroughly. Pour half the batter into greased bundt pan.

Heat the chopped apples in microwave in a 1-cup measure for 2 minutes or until soft. Spoon the apples over batter in bundt pan. Sprinkle half the brown sugar and cinnamon over the apples. Spread remaining batter on top. Sprinkle the remaining brown sugar and cinnamon on top.

Bake for 1 hour. Do not underbake.

Red Gables Inn
Bed & Breakfast

403 North High Street
Lake City, MN 55041
(651)345-2605
(888)345-2605
www.redgablesinn.com
mary@redgablesinn.com

Hosts: Mary & Doug De Roos

Experience the quiet elegance of our Mississippi River Victorian. Built in 1865, this intimate Bed & Breakfast Inn captures the romantic spirit of the Victorian era with a charming mixture of Italianate and Greek Revival architecture. The Inn has been thoughtfully restored to create an inviting ambiance of past splendor and elegance. Individually decorated rooms are appointed with appropriate antiques, reproduction style queen and king size beds and private baths with showers or showers over claw-foot soaking tubs. Ceiling fans bring fresh, cool Lake Pepin breezes in, while air conditioning is available for warmer days. Guests are invited to share the comfort of our parlor, a serene setting for conversation, reading, enjoying games or playing the piano. Prior to dining, complimentary twilight wine and hors d'oeuvres are enjoyed while sharing the camaraderie of new friends in the fireside dining room or on the wraparound porch. Guests will awaken to a savory breakfast buffet of juices, seasonal fruits, home baked breads and pastries, special egg dishes, jams, jellies and coffee and tea.

During your visit, guests can experience a variety of year-round outdoor activities. The scenic splendor of the Hiawatha Valley, Mississippi River bluff land and Lake Pepin make it the perfect place for a leisurely getaway. Our 2-1/2 mile river walk, many parks, beaches and vintage villages offer unique opportunities to explore outdoor activities, shopping, antiquing and much more.

Rates at Red Gables Inn Bed & Breakfast range from $99 to $150.
Rates include a full breakfast.

Bev's Grandmother's Warm Apple Pudding

This recipe was passed down to me from Bev Meyer, who operated the Evergreen Knoll Acres Bed & Breakfast, located just outside of Lake City. Bev chuckled in disbelief at my request for her German grandmother's old family recipe. I had enjoyed a similar dish while my husband and I were stationed in Germany with the U.S. Army. I tried unsuccessfully to get the recipe while we lived there. When I obtained the recipe and began serving it to my family, they were delighted! I serve this recipe as part of a generous breakfast buffet at the Inn. I enjoy preparing this delicious recipe for my guests during our fall apple harvest time and during Lake City's Johnny Appleseed Festival held every October. When I pass on this recipe to the many guest that request it, I smile as I remember my dear friend.

Serves 8

8 medium to large cooking apples – *I use Haralson apples*	9" x 13" x 2" glass baking dish
1/4 cup soft shortening, such as Crisco®	1 mixer with 2-quart bowl or hand mixer with 2-quart bowl
1/2 cup soft butter	1 large mixing bowl
1-1/2 cups granulated sugar	rubber spatula
1-1/2 teaspoons baking powder	2-quart cooking pan with lid
3/4 teaspoon salt	measuring cups and spoons
1 cup milk	hot plate trivet for buffet table
2 teaspoons real vanilla extract	pair of good hot pad holders for transporting pudding
3 egg whites (1/2 cup), unbeaten	
nonstick cooking spray	Baking Time: 45 minutes
	Baking Temperature: 350°

Preheat oven to 350°. Coat glass baking dish with nonstick cooking spray. Peel, core and slice apples; place in glass baking dish; set aside.

In a large mixing bowl, cream together shortening, butter and granulated sugar. In a separate bowl, mix flour, baking powder and salt. Add flour mixture, alternating with milk, to creamed mixture and blend until smooth. Add vanilla and egg whites; blend until smooth. Pour this batter over apples and spread with a spatula until smooth, forcing batter down into sliced apples.Place dish on middle rack of oven and bake for 45 minutes or until a toothpick inserted in center comes out clean. Pudding will become lightly brown on top.

Warm Vanilla Sauce:
- 2 cups water, divided
- 4 Tablespoons cornstarch
- 2 teaspoons real vanilla extract
- 1/4 cup butter
- 2 cups granulated sugar

Dissolve cornstarch in 4 Tablespoons water; set aside. Place remaining water and sugar in 2-quart heavy bottom pan and simmer until all sugar is dissolved. Slowly add dissolved cornstarch while stirring mixture. Cook until mixture begins to thicken and turns clear. Add butter and vanilla; stir until blended. Drizzle 1/2 cup sauce over warm baked pudding. Place remaining sauce in pitcher and serve on the side with pudding.

Hillcrest Hide-Away Bed & Breakfast

404 Hillcrest Street East
Lanesboro, MN 55949
(507)467-3079
(800)697-9902
www.hillcresthideaway.com
hillcresthideaway@yahoo.com

Hosts: Marv & Carol Eggert

Enjoy comfort and peace at the top of lovely Lanesboro, Minnesota. Hillcrest Hide-Away is built in the true Craftsman tradition, with all the original beauty of the architecture and the wood shining through. Four guest rooms, all comfortable seating and private bathrooms, provide the backdrop for a restful night after a day on the 50+ mile bike trail, which doubles as a cross-country ski trail in the winter. All guests are served a hot loaf of homemade bread, followed by a full, hearty breakfast. What a great start for a new day!

Rates at Hillcrest Hide-Away Bed & Breakfast range from $85 to $105.
Rates include a full breakfast.

Genuine Egg Roll

This recipe is so easy! It tastes so good, too! It looks pretty and impressive. What more can you want for breakfast?

Serves 6

12 eggs
1/2 teaspoon salt
1/4 teaspoon pepper

Filling:
2 teaspoons honey mustard, approximately
1/2 pound thinly sliced ham
1/2 pound grated cheese of your choice
1/2 cup thinly sliced green onion

1 medium mixing bowl
10" x 15" baking sheet or jelly roll pan
parchment or wax paper
aluminum foil

Baking Time: 20 minutes, divided
Baking Temperature: 350°

Preheat oven to 350°. Lightly grease baking sheet. Line with greased parchment or wax paper. In a medium mixing bowl, beat eggs, salt and pepper. Pour into prepared pan and bake for 10-15 minutes or until set.

When eggs are set, remove pan from oven and invert onto a large piece of aluminum foil. Spread a thin layer of mustard on baked eggs. Layer with meat and cheese. Top with onions.

Roll up, starting at long edge, just like a jelly roll. Wrap in foil. Place gently on pan and return to oven for 10 minutes.

Remove from oven. Unwrap. Cut into slices and place cut side up on warmed plate.

Chai Scones

These scones combine the mysterious flavor of chai with the familiar texture of a scone. There are many instant chai powders on the market. Don't confuse them with brewed chai tea.

Makes 8 scones

1-1/2 cups flour
1/4 cup sugar
1/4 teaspoon baking soda
1-1/4 teaspoons baking powder
1/4 teaspoon salt
4 Tablespoons instant chai powder, divided
1/3 cup cold butter, cut into small pieces
1 teaspoon grated orange peel
1/2 cup buttermilk

1 medium mixing bowl
pastry blender
baking sheet

Baking Time: 12 minutes
Baking Temperature: 425°

Preheat oven to 425°. Place dry ingredients (which includes 3 Tablespoons of chai powder) in medium mixing bowl and mix thoroughly. Using a pastry blender or 2 knives, cut butter into flour mixture until it is coarse. Do not over mix. Add orange peel. Add buttermilk and mix until dough leaves the side of the bowl. Knead a couple of times until smooth.

Place on lightly greased baking sheet and form into a circle about 8" in diameter. Score, but do not separate into 8 wedges. Sprinkle top with remaining chai powder.

Bake for 12 minutes. Serve immediately.

Grandma's Cut Out Cookies

These are the cookies Grandma always made for my sister and me when we would come to visit. Even though they are a bit "putsy," they will melt in your mouth. Just don't over mix them. That will make them tough. Our guests love them in the cookie jar!

Makes about 3 dozen cookies

3	cups flour
1/2	cup shortening
1/2	cup butter or margarine
1	teaspoon baking soda
1/2	teaspoon cream of tartar
3	egg yolks
1/4	cup milk
1	cup sugar
1	teaspoon vanilla
	flour for rolling out dough
	colored sugars for decoration

1	small mixing bowl
1	large mixing bowl
	electric mixer
	whisk
	fun shaped cookie cutters
	baking sheets

Baking Time: 8-10 minutes
Baking Temperature: 350°

Preheat oven to 350°. In a large mixing bowl, sift together flour, baking soda and cream of tartar. Cut in butter or margarine until mixture is coarse. Do not over mix. In a small mixing bowl, combine egg yolks, milk, sugar and vanilla. Add wet mixture gently to the dry mixture. Mix just until blended. Cool.

Roll a small amount of dough on to a lightly floured board, using a lightly floured rolling pin. Using cookie cutters of your choice, cut dough and place cookies gently on ungreased baking or cookie sheets. Decorate with colored sugars.

Bake for 8-10 minutes. Remove to wire rack for cooling.

Historic Scanlan House Bed & Breakfast Inn

708 Parkway Avenue South
Lanesboro, MN 55949
(507)467-2158
(800)944-2158
www.ScanlanHouse.com
ScanlanBB@aol.com

Host: Kirsten Lee Mensing

The Historic Scanlan House Bed & Breakfast Inn offers its guests a full day and night of peaceful serenity. We offer five elegant guest bedrooms, all furnished with antiques. Each room also has a small color television and air conditioning. You can enjoy our graceful surroundings by sitting on the front porch and watching the occasional Amish horse and buggy go by, or by taking advantage of our beautiful patio. You can play a challenging game of chess or even croquet on the front lawn. After a long day of biking, rollerblading, golfing, canoeing or tubing, you can enjoy one of our many current movie selections and/or a glass of Irish Cream in our front parlor or library. Maybe you would prefer to retire to your bedroom and sip complimentary champagne in front of the fireplace or relax in your whirlpool. Enjoy our famous five-course delectable breakfast – a delight to the eye and to the taste buds. While visiting Lanesboro and Historic Scanlan House Bed & Breakfast Inn, we are certain you will enjoy yourself.

Rates at Historic Scanlan House Bed & Breakfast Inn range from $90 to $225.
Rates include a full breakfast.

Mom's Apple Cranberry Corn Bread with Honey Butter

This is best served warm with the scrumptious honey butter. An easy and delicious recipe!

Makes 10 servings

1 cup yellow cornmeal
1 cup all-purpose flour
1/4 cup sugar
1 teaspoon baking soda
1 teaspoon baking powder
3/4 teaspoon salt
1 cup buttermilk
1 egg
1/4 cup corn oil
1 cup green apple, peeled, cored
   and coarsely chopped
1/2 cup dried cranberries
1 medium mixing bowl
1 large mixing bowl
   8" x 8" square baking pan

Baking Time: 35-40 minutes
Baking Temperature: 350°

Preheat oven to 350°. Mix all dry ingredients together in a large mixing bowl until blended. In a medium mixing bowl, beat egg; whisk in buttermilk and corn oil. Stir this mixture into the dry mixture until completely moistened. Stir in apples and cranberries. Spread evenly in greased pan.

Bake for 35-40 minutes or until a fork inserted in the center comes out clean. Cool slightly in pan before cutting into squares. Serve with honey butter, listed below.

Honey butter:
   2 sticks (1 cup) butter, softened
   1/2 cup honey

With a spoon, blend butter and honey together. Mix thoroughly but not to the point of runniness. If that should occur, pop it into the freezer for about 5 minutes.

Quick & Easy Apple and Coconut Crisp

This unusual crisp will be sure to leave your guests asking for the recipe! It is best served warm with vanilla or cinnamon ice cream.

Makes 8-10 servings

Crust and Crumble Topping:
- 2 cups flour
- 1 cup sugar
- 2 sticks (1 cup) butter

Filling:
- 5-6 medium apples, peeled, cored and sliced or chunked
- 1/2 cup uncooked oatmeal
- 3/4 cup shredded sweetened or unsweetened coconut
- 1 cup brown sugar
- 1/2 cup sugar
- 2 Tablespoons cinnamon
- 1 teaspoon ground clove
- 1 teaspoon ground nutmeg
- 1 cup raisins, optional

- 2 large mixing bowls
- 9" x 13" baking pan

Baking Time: 35 minutes, divided
Baking Temperature: 350°

Preheat oven to 350°.

Topping:
Melt butter in microwave for approximately 1 minute. Add flour and sugar. Mix together with spoon until blended. Use 3/4 of the mixture to form a crust on the bottom of baking pan. For a thicker crisp, use a smaller pan. Bake for 10 minutes; remove from oven.

Filling:
Peel and core apples: either slice or chunk them and place in large mixing bowl. Combine all ingredients, using large mixing spoons or spatulas to mix ingredients together. Evenly spread apple and coconut filling over the precooked crust. Sprinkle remaining topping over filling. Bake for approximately 25 minutes or until golden brown and slightly bubbling at the sides.

Vanilla and Cinnamon Poached Pears in Caramel and Clove Crème Sauce

This recipe is wonderful any time of the day! If you wish to make 12 servings instead of 6, cut pears in half and fan slices on the plate.

Makes 6 servings

Poached Pears:
- 6 ripe medium pears
- 2 fresh cinnamon sticks
- 1/8 cup real vanilla extract
- 3-1/2 cups water
- 1-1/2 cups sugar

Sauce:
- 2 egg yolks, beaten
- 2 Tablespoons water
- 1/4 cup sugar
- 3 Tablespoons Torani brand caramel syrup
- 2 teaspoons ground cloves
- 1 cup whipping cream
  fresh mint, optional
  raspberries, optional
  melted chocolate, optional

- medium saucepan
- double boiler
- 2 small mixing bowls
- electric mixer

To poach pears, in a medium saucepan, bring 3-1/2 cups water, cinnamon sticks, vanilla and 1-1/2 cups sugar to boiling. Carefully add pears, stem ends up. Reduce heat. Cover and simmer for about 20 minutes or until pears are tender. Remove saucepan from heat and let pears cool in liquid.

Sauce:
In the top of a double boiler, thoroughly combine egg yolks, water and sugar. Place the top of the double boiler over, but not touching, gently boiling water. Beat with an electric mixer on medium speed for about 10 minutes or until mixture is very thick, fluffy and pale yellow. Remove from heat; transfer to a small mixing bowl. Immediately stir in caramel syrup. Let cool for about 10 minutes. Wash mixer. In another small mixing bowl, beat whipping cream until stiff peaks form. Fold whipped cream into egg yolk mixture.

To serve, remove pears from liquid and drain well. Spoon some of the sauce onto dessert plates. Place pears on top of the sauce, then spoon remaining sauce over pears. Garnish stem of pear with mint and, if desired, garnish plate with raspberries and melted chocolate.

Sauce Shortcut:
If you don't have time to cook the sauce, use this very simple and quick shortcut: Using 1 large tube (12 ounces) of Cool Whip, hand stir in 3 Tablespoons of caramel syrup and cloves. Instead of melting chocolate, lightly drizzle Hershey® Chocolate Syrup over the crème mixture on plate.

Historic Rand House
Bed & Breakfast

506 Territorial Road
Monticello, MN 55362
(763)295-6037
www.randhouse.com
info@randhouse.com

Hosts: Duffy & Merrill Busch

On a hilltop overlooking downtown Monticello, Random is the historic summer country estate of Mr. and Mrs. Rufus Rand, Sr. At its center stands The Rand House, a wedding gift from Rufus to his bride, Susan, in 1884. Listed on the National Register of Historic Places, The Rand House has been totally restored and now offers four guest rooms, each with a private bath and several with fireplaces. Guests may enjoy the winter parlor with its massive stone fireplace, the solarium filled with greenery, or the drawing room with grand piano and fireplace. Surrounding the house are sweeping lawns, offering hilltop views of the city and woods. Golf, antiquing, shopping, cross-country skiing, hiking, biking and bird watching are just minutes away. Breakfast is served in the solarium, the dining room or the wraparound screened porch. Escape to a romantic past…just 40 minutes from downtown Minneapolis, but more than 100 years away!

Rates at Historic Rand House Bed & Breakfast range from $115 to $175.
Rates include a full breakfast.

Strawberry-Coconut Scones

These delightful scones are perfect for breakfast or any time that you want to impress your guests!

Serves 8

1-3/4 cups all-purpose flour
1 cup sweetened flaked coconut
1/4 cup sugar
1 Tablespoon baking powder
1 Tablespoon grated lemon peel
1/2 teaspoon salt
3/4 cup heavy cream
2 large eggs
1 pint (12 ounces) strawberries, diced
2 Tablespoons sugar

1 large mixing bowl
1 small mixing bowl
14" baking sheet

Baking Time: 30-35 minutes
Baking Temperature: 375°

Preheat oven to 375°. Coat large baking sheet with nonstick cooking spray.

In a large mixing bowl, combine flour, coconut, sugar, baking powder, lemon peel and salt. In a small mixing bowl, blend cream and eggs. Pour cream mixture over flour mixture; add strawberries and stir until mixed and dough clumps together. Scrape onto center of prepared sheet. Pat into a 9" round (dough will be sticky). Sprinkle with sugar. Coat a long knife with nonstick cooking spray; cut round into 8 wedges; don't separate the wedges. Dough can also be scooped onto baking sheet with ice cream scoop for individual scones. This method will produce 8-10 scones.

Bake for 30 minutes until puffed and well browned and a wooden toothpick inserted in center comes out clean. Strawberries will caramelize on baking sheet.

Cut wedges again. Serve warm or at room temperature. Top with fresh whipped cream and a sprinkle of coconut or fanned strawberry for garnish.

Deutsche Strasse
Bed & Breakfast

404 South German Street
New Ulm, MN 56073
(507)354-2005
(866)226-9856
www.deutschestrasse.com
info@deutschstrasse.com

Hosts: Gary & Ramona Sonnenberg

Come, visit the city of charm and tradition while relaxing in the comforts of home at the Deutsche Strasse Bed & Breakfast. We treat you like gold with our relaxing atmosphere, cozy rooms, private baths and comfortable beds, and by serving a four-course breakfast to you in the morning. Since 1998, Gary and Ramona have shared their graciously preserved 1884 historic home, offering genuine hospitality and charming accommodations of a home built during the golden era of New Ulm and renovated in 1915 with the influence of the Arts and Crafts movement of Frank Lloyd Wright.

Relax and feel the calmness of a time past; our four rooms on the main level invite you to sit back and let the world pass you by. A baby grand piano is available for those who wish to play; an all-season sun porch is the perfect place to curl up with a good book or a glass of fine wine; a picturesque living room, with a candlelit marble fireplace and a 55-gallon aquarium, is the ultimate in relaxation after a busy day enjoying the attractions of New Ulm. Some of the many attractions include: Morgan Creek Vineyards; August Schell Brewery; the Minnesota Music Hall of Fame; and the Brown County Historical Museum. Outdoor enthusiasts will enjoy Flandrau State Park for swimming, hiking and groomed cross-country ski trails; plus golfing, biking, and many other outdoor activities are within close range. Don't forget to visit the many great shops and restaurants. Our quaint town is only two hours from Minneapolis, St. Cloud or Rochester.

Escape, explore and rejuvenate!

Rates at Deutsche Strasse Bed & Breakfast range from $69 to $94.
Rates include a full breakfast.

Berry & Nut Granola

At the Deutsche Strasse Bed & Breakfast, we serve homemade granolas as our first course at breakfast. Many of our guests have requested these recipes or look forward to their return to Deutsche Strasse B & B to be able to enjoy more. This recipe takes some time to prepare, but the fresh taste is worth the effort. The granola also keeps well in the refrigerator for a month.

Makes 7 cups

4 cups old-fashioned oats
1 cup nonfat dry milk powder
1/2 cup walnuts, chopped
1/4 cup wheat germ
1 Tablespoon ground cinnamon
3/4 cup packed brown sugar
1/4 cup water
1/2 cup vegetable oil
1 teaspoon vanilla extract
1 cup dried berry mix
1/2 cup raisins
  nonstick cooking spray

1 large mixing bowl
  15" x 10" baking pan
  measuring cups and spoons
  medium saucepan
2 large spoons for stirring

Baking Time: 1 hour 15 minutes
Baking Temperature: 275°

Preheat oven to 275°. In a large mixing bowl, combine oats, milk powder, walnuts, wheat germ and cinnamon. Stir with large spoon to mix.

In a medium saucepan over medium heat, bring brown sugar and water to a boil, stirring with spoon. Remove from heat; stir in oil and vanilla until mixed. Pour over oat mixture and stir until evenly moistened.

Pour into a greased baking pan. Bake for 1 hour, stirring every 15 minutes. The mixture should be turning a golden brown. Stir in the dried berry mix and bake another 15 minutes.

Remove from oven and stir in raisins. Cool, stirring occasionally. Store in airtight container in the refrigerator. We serve this granola as a cereal with milk or vanilla yogurt. Enjoy it by itself or over fresh fruit pieces.

Hundred Acre Woods Bed & Breakfast

5048 Old Highway 53
Orr, MN 55771
(218)757-0070
www.voyageurcountry.com/hundredacrewoods
bnb@rangenet.com

Hosts: Veronica Holman, Drew Holman & Jacob Holman

H undred Acre Woods Bed & Breakfast is nestled in the Northern Minnesota forests. It is a homey and comforting place from which to enjoy adventures in Minnesota's theatre of seasons. There are many lakes within a 30-mile radius to enjoy, whether you are fishing, swimming, canoeing, boating or just enjoying the beauty. Autumn is especially exhilarating in the northland with its clean, cool air and spectacular color, inviting you to take a brisk walk. The Bed & Breakfast is adjacent to the Orr snowmobile trail, which connects to other trails that will eventually take you to Voyageurs National Park and Canada. Hiking, cross-country skiing and snowshoeing trails are nearby as well. A favorite summer activity is visiting the Vince Shute Bear Sanctuary, where you can safely view bears in their natural habitat.

At day's end, imagine yourself relaxing in a cozy woodland setting after a day of outdoor activity. To pamper you further, a therapeutic massage can be arranged. Then, when you rise, you will be enticed by the warm aromas of a northwoods gourmet breakfast from Veronica's kitchen.

Whether you stay for a day or a week, come up to the northwoods and enjoy the hospitality at the Hundred Acre Woods Bed & Breakfast and romance the nature in you.

Rates at Hundred Acre Woods Bed & Breakfast range from $79.95 to $169.95.
Rates include a full breakfast.

Wild Rice Salad

This recipe is always a hit! Folks just seem to love the nutty, unique wild rice taste. We made this salad as one of the dishes for the guests at my daughter Heather's wedding reception. We made two versions of the salad – one with chicken and one with no meat for those who prefer vegetarian fare. Wild rice is a favorite in Northern Minnesota, where it is harvested every fall. In addition to being tasty, this salad is also very nutritious.

Serves 5-6

        1   cup wild rice, cooked
        1   teaspoon salt
      1/2   teaspoon pepper
      2/3   cup mayonnaise
        1   teaspoon lemon juice
      1/4   cup yellow onion, finely chopped
        1   cup green grapes
        1   cup red grapes
        1   cup nuts (cashews, almonds or walnuts)
        1   can (8 ounces) water chestnuts
        2   cups cooked and cubed chicken, optional

        1   large mixing bowl
            6-quart saucepan
            3-quart bowl for serving

   In saucepan, cook wild rice; drain and cool. In a large mixing bowl, combine salt, pepper, mayonnaise, lemon juice and onion. Add grapes and nuts. Add chicken, if desired. Gently mix in wild rice.

   Refrigerate for 1 hour before serving. Salad may be garnished with lettuce, edible flowers (nasturtiums, pansies), parsley or mint.

Bread Pudding with Whiskey Sauce

My oldest son, Ryan, commented on this recipe at a gathering: "The sauce is so good you drink it by itself."

Serves 5-6

4 eggs	1 medium mixing bowl
2 cups milk	2-quart saucepan
1/3 cup sugar	8" x 8" baking dish
1/2 teaspoon cinnamon	saucepan
1/2 teaspoon vanilla	
3 cups dry bread cubes (4 slices) or I substitute Potica* for the bread and don't add the fruit	Baking Time: 35-40 minutes
	Baking Temperature: 325°
1/3 cup raisins or snipped dried fruit	

Potica is a walnut pastry that was brought into my family by my grandmother Maria when she came to Minnesota from Slovenia.

Preheat oven to 325°. In a medium mixing bowl, beat eggs; add milk, sugar, cinnamon and vanilla. Place dry bread cubes in baking dish. Sprinkle fruit over bread. Pour egg mixture over all ingredients. Bake for 35-40 minutes or until knife inserted in pudding comes out clean. Cool pudding slightly, then serve with whiskey sauce.

Whiskey Sauce:
1/4 cup butter
1/2 cup sugar
1 beaten egg yolk
2 Tablespoons water
2 Tablespoons whiskey

Mix all ingredients in a saucepan, stirring constantly until sugar dissolves and mixture comes to a boil. Cool the sauce slightly and pour over bread pudding. Enjoy!

Cucumber Cream Cheese Appetizer

I especially like this recipe because it's quick, simple and very tasty. It is welcomed by guests as an evening appetizer.

Serves 10-12

8 ounces cream cheese
2 teaspoons dry zesty Italian
    salad dressing
1-2 cucumbers
1 teaspoon dill weed
    cocktail pumpernickel bread

1 medium mixing bowl

In a medium mixing bowl, mix cream cheese and dry Italian dressing. Let set for 20 minutes. Spread on pumpernickel bread. Slice cucumber and put slices on cream cheese mixture. Sprinkle with dill weed.

LoonSong
Bed & Breakfast

17248 Loon Song Lane
Lake Itasca #27
Park Rapids, MN 56470
(218)266-3333
(888)825-8135
www.loonsongbedandbreakfast.com
loonsong@arvig.net

Hosts: Barb & Dennis Cowan

An exceptional wilderness getaway, LoonSong is located on beautiful Heart Lake, just six miles from Itasca State Park and the headwaters of the Mississippi River. At LoonSong, you can hike, bike, boat, swim, ski or play fetch with the dogs. Or you may choose to just wander along the lake eating raspberries, sit in the garden with a book, curl up in front of the fireplace or take a nap in a queen-size bed with fluffy pillows. LoonSong's four guest rooms are furnished with antiques and full private baths. Each room opens onto its own deck or patio. Mornings start with coffee, tea and muffins delivered to your door, followed by a full gourmet breakfast with Barb later in the morning. Located in the center of the Itasca area lakes, LoonSong is close to several biking, skiing and snowmobiling trails and golf courses. The food is great, the company is fine, and the beautiful split-log home setting on this quiet Northwoods lake is unparalleled.

Rates at LoonSong Bed & Breakfast range from $79 to $129.
Rates include a full breakfast.

Raspberry French Toast

Raspberry French Toast is easy to make, wonderfully delicious to eat and looks sumptuous as you serve your guests. Make the night before, refrigerate and just bake the next morning.

Makes 6 servings

12 slices Texas Toast white
    bread
1 cup raspberries, fresh or
    frozen, thawed
3 eggs
3/4 cup half-and-half
8 Tablespoons butter, melted
1/3 cup raspberry jam
    powdered sugar
    whipped cream

9" x 13" glass baking dish
1 medium mixing bowl

Baking Time: 20-25 minutes
Baking Temperature: 425°

Spray baking dish with nonstick cooking spray. Butter one side of slice of bread with melted butter and place butter side down in pan. Spread raspberry jam on second piece of bread and place jam side down on top of other slice. Brush melted butter on top of slice.

In a medium mixing bowl, mix slightly beaten eggs and half-and-half together. Pour evenly over all slices in pan. Cover with foil and refrigerate overnight.

Preheat oven to 425°. Bake for 20-25 minutes or until top is golden brown. Serve warm from the oven. Place on warm plate dusted with powdered sugar, pile whipped cream in center and sprinkle raspberries on top. Garnish with a sprig of mint. Warm maple syrup and raspberry syrup in small pitchers to serve on the side.

Fabulous Variations:
Strawberry French Toast-
Spread strawberry jam on bread. Slice one package of strawberries or thawed frozen strawberries in bowl, drizzle with warm honey and let stand until ready to serve. Serve with warm strawberry syrup in small pitchers.

Peach French Toast-
Spread peach preserves on bread. Slice one peach per person in bowl, sprinkle with lemon juice and a dash of nutmeg. Let stand until ready to serve. Serve with warm peach or apricot syrup in small pitchers.

Prairie View Estate

43581 County Highway 9
Pelican Rapids, MN 56572
(218)863-4321
(800)298-8058
www.prairieviewestate.com
prairie@prtel.com

Hosts: Phyllis & Lyle Haugrud

Prairie View Estate is a charming 1927 Scandinavian home on a country estate, nestled in the trees on 300 acres just one mile north of Pelican Rapids. Family heirlooms decorate the three cozy bedrooms as well as the sunny four-season porch, quiet parlor and country dining room. The three bedrooms, all with private baths, are named after the owner's mother, Tillie, her Uncle Edwin, and the Hired Men (which has a whirlpool bath). This quiet and serene Bed & Breakfast will make you feel at home while being pampered. Awaken to the sound of birds singing and smells of a delicious breakfast featuring a special French Toast or egg soufflés, served in the antique-filled dining room or on the porch. Located nearby are many lakes, golf courses, antique shops, gift shops and Maplewood State Park for summer hiking and biking and winter snowmobiling and cross-country skiing.

Experience the serenity!

Rates at Prairie View Estate range from $70 to $85.
Rates include a full breakfast.

Rhubarb Crunch Muffins

This is a moist and tender muffin that goes great with an egg dish or just on its own. It is an easy to prepare recipe. Our guests love them!

Makes 24 medium or 12 jumbo muffins

Muffins:
1-1/2 cups brown sugar
2-1/2 cups flour
1 teaspoon salt
1 teaspoon baking soda
1/2 teaspoon cinnamon
2/3 cup Crisco® oil
1 egg, slightly beaten
1 cup buttermilk
2 cups rhubarb, finely cut
1 teaspoon vanilla

Topping:
1/2 cup sugar
1 Tablespoon butter, melted
1 teaspoon cinnamon
Mix together and sprinkle over tops of muffins.

1 small mixing bowl
1 large mixing bowl
   greased or paper lined
      muffin tins

Baking Time: 20-25 minutes
Baking Temperature: 350°

Preheat oven to 350°. In a large mixing bowl, combine dry ingredients – sugar, flour, salt, baking soda and cinnamon. In a small mixing bowl, beat egg and add oil, buttermilk and vanilla. Add egg mixture to dry ingredients, then add rhubarb. Combine only until moistened; do not over mix.

Divide evenly among muffin tins. Sprinkle with topping. Bake for 20-25 minutes or until tops of muffins are a light golden brown.

Another great recipe from Prairie View Estate:

Graham Streusel Cake

This coffee cake is a favorite with our guests when served with coffee or tea…or even with their breakfast!

Makes 12-15 servings

Cake:
> 2 cups graham cracker crumbs
> 3/4 cup chopped nuts – walnuts or pecans
> 3/4 cup brown sugar
> 1-1/4 teaspoon cinnamon
> 3/4 cup melted butter
> 1 cup water
> 1/4 cup vegetable oil
> 3 eggs
> 1 package yellow cake mix (or your favorite flavor)

Glaze:
> 1 cup powdered sugar
> 1-2 Tablespoons water or milk
> 1 Tablespoon melted butter

Mix together all ingredients and drizzle over cake when cool.

> 1 medium mixing bowl
> 1 large mixing bowl
> mixer
> 9" x 13" pan

Baking Time: 45-50 minutes
Baking Temperature: 350°

Preheat oven to 350°.

In a medium mixing bowl, mix together graham cracker crumbs, nuts, brown sugar, cinnamon and butter. Reserve. In a large mixing bowl, blend cake mix, water, oil and eggs on low speed. Beat on medium speed for 3 minutes.

Pour half of the cake batter into pan. Sprinkle with half of the crumb mixture. Pour remaining cake batter over crumb mixture, then top with remaining crumb mixture.

Bake for 45-50 minutes or until toothpick inserted in center comes out clean. Drizzle glaze over cooled cake.

Banana Bread

This is an old family recipe handed down from my sister. It is moist and delicious and very easy to make, and guests of all ages love it. I added chocolate chips, also, and it is very good!

Makes 16 servings

1/2 cup butter or margarine
1 cup sugar
2 eggs
2 Tablespoons milk
1 teaspoon baking soda
1/4 cup warm water
2 bananas, crushed
2 cups flour
1/2 teaspoon salt

1 small mixing bowl
1 large mixing bowl
mixer
9" x 5" loaf pan

Baking Time: about 1 hour
Baking Temperature: 350°

Preheat oven to 350°. In a large mixing bowl, cream together butter and sugar. Add eggs and milk.

In a small mixing bowl, dissolve baking soda in warm water; add to butter mixture. Add crushed bananas and mix. Add flour and salt and beat just until mixed. Do not over mix.

Pour in loaf pan and bake for about 1 hour or until toothpick inserted in center comes out clean.

Candlelight Inn

818 West 3rd Street
Red Wing, MN 55066
(651)388-8034
(800)254-9194
www.candlelightinn-redwing.com
candlerw@charter.net

Hosts: Lynette & Zig Gudrais

The Candlelight Inn in Red Wing is a lovely Victorian residence preserved much as it was in 1877. It was built by Horace Rich, the president of The Red Wing Stoneware Company. The authentic Italianate-style home reflects the gentility and charm of the Victorian era, updated with modern conveniences. All five rooms have fireplaces, and three rooms have whirlpool bathtubs.

The Inn is three blocks from Red Wing's renowned downtown, making it the perfect starting point for a shopping excursion, a stroll on the Mississippi levee or flower-basket-lined streets. Our unique shops and great restaurants are all within walking distance. For those seeking a romantic getaway or a special getaway, the Candlelight Inn is the perfect place to stay.

Rates at Candlelight Inn range from $109 to $199.
Rates include a full breakfast.

Orange French Toast

This is our most frequently requested recipe. It can be made the night before or 2 hours before baking. It fills the Inn with the unbeatable aroma of cinnamon and orange mingling with the freshly ground and brewed coffee. What a beautiful morning!

Serves 4

1/4 cup melted butter
1/3 cup sugar mixed with 1 teaspoon cinnamon
  1 teaspoon orange peel
  4 eggs, beaten
2/3 cup orange juice
  2 Tablespoons Grand Marnier liqueur, optional
  8 slices (1/2" thick) Italian bread

    15" x 10" jelly roll pan
  1 large mixing bowl

Baking Time: 25 minutes
Baking Temperature: 400°

Melt butter and pour into jelly roll pan. Sprinkle sugar-cinnamon mixture over butter evenly. Sprinkle orange peel over sugar mixture evenly.

In a large mixing bowl, mix eggs, orange juice and Grand Marnier well. Dip bread in mixture, one slice at a time, soaking well. Put bread in pan and spoon any extra mixture over bread. Cover and refrigerate overnight or for 2 hours.

Preheat oven to 400°. Bake in preheated oven for 25 minutes. Let stand for 1 minute. Flip sugar side up to serve. Serve with apricot or maple syrup.

Champagne Pears with Vanilla Custard Sauce

An elegant ending to any dinner, a prelude to brunch, or a stand-alone dessert, this is our premium recipe. People always enjoy guessing what's in it, and there's never any left over.

Serves 12

6 ripe red Anjou pears
   (or any variety – these
   are the best)
1/2 cup almonds, any variety
1/2 cup walnuts
1/2 – 3/4 cup sugar
1 egg
2 cups champagne or red
   wine or combination

16" x 11" Pyrex baking dish or any
   large, shallow baking dish
food processor

Baking Time: 1 hour
Baking Temperature: 400°

Preheat oven to 400°. Pare pears. Cut in half vertically, from stem to blossom end. Using melon baler, scoop out the center core. With small, sharp paring knife, cut out and discard the vein leading to the stem. Then scoop out two more small melon-ball portions of pear on either side of the center and reserve. Cut a thin slice off the bottom of each half so pears will sit evenly in pan. Reserve these slices with other reserved pear.

Place all pear halves in large baking dish. Put reserved pear, egg, 1/4 cup sugar and both kinds of nuts in the work bowl of a food processor. Using pulses, process until almost smooth. Fill cavities in pears with mixture. Sprinkle remaining sugar over top of pears. Pour wine into dish, not covering and not on top of pears.

Place on bottom rack of preheated oven for 1 hour. When done, cool slightly. Put into stemmed dessert dish with a little wine sauce. Spoon vanilla custard sauce (below) over top, about 2 Tablespoons. Sprinkle with a few chopped, toasted almonds, if you wish.

Vanilla Custard Sauce:
1 package (5 ounces) instant vanilla pudding mix
2 cups whole milk
1 cup half-and-half

Prepare pudding mix as package directs, using 3 cups liquid as indicated above instead of 2 cups milk. Refrigerate for at least 10 minutes.

Cherry-Chocolate Cookies

We have several great cookies waiting with milk or coffee when folks return to the Inn in the evening. This is a favorite.

Makes 1 dozen large cookies

1	cup dried cherries
1	cup boiling water
1	stick (1/2 cup) softened butter
1/2	cup sugar
1/2	cup packed brown sugar
1	large egg
2	teaspoons vanilla
1-1/2	cups flour
1/2	teaspoon baking soda
1/4	teaspoon salt
3/4	cup white chocolate chips
1/2	cup milk chocolate chips
1/2	cup chopped pecans

1	small mixing bowl
1	large mixing bowl
	electric mixer
	cookie sheet or baking stone

Baking Time: 13-15 minutes
Baking Temperature: 350°

Preheat oven to 350°. Place dried cherries in small mixing bowl. Cover with boiling water. Let stand 5 minutes. Drain. Set aside.

In a large mixing bowl, combine butter and sugars. Beat for 2 minutes. Add egg and vanilla; beat. Beat in flour, baking soda and salt. Mix in cherries, chocolate chips and pecans.

Drop onto cookie sheets by scoop, 4" apart. Bake for 13-15 minutes, rotating cookie sheet halfway through baking.

Cool on wire racks.

The Chatsworth
Bed & Breakfast

984 Ashland Avenue
St. Paul, MN 55104
(651)227-4288
(866)978-4837
www.chatsworth-bb.com
chats@isd.net

Hosts: Heather & Justin Johnson

Ideally situated in the heart of St. Paul's Summit University neighborhood, The Chatsworth Bed & Breakfast's superb location offers guests the option of exploring Saint Paul on foot, or if they prefer, by car. Guests are invited to stroll along the renowned Summit Avenue – just two blocks south – and marvel at the beauty of the longest stretch of preserved Victorian homes in America. Just one block farther is Grand Avenue, a lengthy outdoor boulevard home to unique specialty shops, fine restaurants and quaint cafes. Whatever the desire or pace, the staff of The Chatsworth Bed & Breakfast are all devoted to helping our guests discover the charms that make Saint Paul such a special place. Open year-round, we invite guests to sample the seasons with us. We are certain all will enjoy living, if only for a short while, in our charming and historic neighborhood.

Rates at The Chatsworth Bed & Breakfast range from $100 to $180.
Rates include a full breakfast.

Chocolate Chip Cookies

I know that everyone has a chocolate chip cookie recipe that they love – but this is by far the best recipe we have ever tasted, and our guests agree! Moist, chewy and "bumpy," these cookies are so popular that we have to make over a dozen a day, and I have had to print up special cards with the recipe because I was writing it down so much! With or without coconut, they are divine!!

Makes 1-1/2 dozen cookies

2-1/2 cups flour
1 cup brown sugar
1/2 cup sugar
1/2 teaspoon baking soda
1 stick (1/2 cup) butter
1/2 cup Crisco® shortening
2 eggs
1-1/2 cups chocolate chips
1-1/4 cups coconut

1 medium mixing bowl
1 large mixing bowl
mixer with paddle attachment
cookie sheet
measuring cups and spoons

Baking Time: 8-10 minutes
Baking Temperature: 325°

Preheat oven to 325° (375° for a radiant oven). Melt butter in microwave or in saucepan over medium heat.

In a large mixing bowl, place eggs and both sugars. Add melted butter and cream together. Add Crisco® and mix until batter is light-colored and smooth.

In a medium mixing bowl, sift together flour and baking soda. Add to smooth mixture 1/2 cup at a time, mixing well between each 1/2 cup. Add chocolate chips and coconut.

Drop by the spoonful onto ungreased cookie sheet. Bake for 8-10 minutes. Cookies should look underdone and light, but not runny, when they are removed from oven. The lighter they are, the chewier they are!! (Which, of course, is our trademark!)

Apricot Pecan Bread

By far our most popular quick bread, this recipe is the perfect accompaniment for a fall or winter brunch. Prior to introducing this bread to our menu, we would slice an entire loaf of quick bread to serve at breakfast. However, this particular bread has a tendency to completely disappear – even if we are only serving a few guests!! Now we serve by the slice, but more often than not, we wrap up extra slices for "later." Praised by the health conscious for its focus on grains, organic fruit and wheat flour, it is definitely worth the extra effort!

Makes approximately 10 slices

- 1 **cup dried organic apricots**
- 1 **cup sugar**
- 1 **cup quick cooking oats**
- 3/4 **cup whole wheat flour**
- 1/4 **cup cake flour**
- 2 **teaspoons baking powder**
- 1/2 **teaspoon baking soda**
- 1/2 **cup orange juice**
- 1 **egg**
- 2 **Tablespoons vegetable oil**
- 1 **cup chopped pecans**

- 1 **large mixing bowl**
- **wooden spoon**
- **medium saucepan**
- **glass loaf pan**

Baking Time: 60-70 minutes
Baking Temperature: 350°

Preheat oven to 350°. Grease glass loaf pan. In saucepan, place apricots and add enough water to just cover apricots. Simmer on medium-high for approximately 15 minutes or until apricots are plump. Drain and cool for 15 minutes, then chop into 1-inch pieces.

In a large mixing bowl, combine dry ingredient. Stir in orange juice, egg and vegetable oil. Batter will be thick. Fold in apricots and pecans.

Transfer batter to greased pan. Bake 60-70 minutes or until edges are dark brown and slightly crispy. Center may sag slightly.

Lemon Poppy Seed Waffles with Blueberry Sauce

If you are looking for a made-from-scratch waffle recipe that not only makes quite a statement, but is simple and delicious, too, then this is the recipe for you! Made most frequently in the summer months because of its refreshing flavor, this recipe has been requested again and again by our guests. Garnish with edible pansies and you have a breakfast fit for a picture!

Serves 4

1-1/2 cups flour	1 small mixing bowl
6 Tablespoons sugar	1 large mixing bowl
2 Tablespoons poppy seeds	whisk
1-1/2 teaspoons baking powder	wooden spoon
1 teaspoon baking soda	waffle iron
2 eggs	ladle
1-1/4 cups buttermilk	saucepan
1/4 cup melted butter	
1 Tablespoon grated lemon peel	

In a large mixing bowl, whisk first 6 ingredients to blend. In a small mixing bowl, whisk eggs, buttermilk, butter and lemon peel. Add buttermilk mixture all at once to flour mixture and whisk just until blended. Let mixture stand for 15 minutes.

Preheat waffle iron according to manufacturer's instructions. Spoon batter onto waffle iron. Cover and cook until golden and cooked through, about 7 minutes. (Cooking time will vary, depending on waffle iron.) Repeat with remaining batter. Serve immediately with warm blueberry sauce.

Blueberry Sauce:
   1 pound frozen blueberries, thawed, not drained
   1/2 cup plus 2 Tablespoons apple juice, divided
   1/2 cup sugar
   1 Tablespoon cornstarch
   1 Tablespoon lemon juice

Bring blueberries, 1/2 cup apple juice and sugar to boil in heavy medium saucepan. Simmer over medium heat until reduced to 2 cups, about 15 minutes. Dissolve cornstarch in remaining 2 Tablespoons apple juice and add to blueberry mixture. Add lemon juice. Bring to boil, stirring constantly; simmer until thick, about 1 minute. Cool slightly before serving. (This can be made 2 days ahead of time. Cover and refrigerate. Warm over medium-low heat before serving.)

The Covington Inn
Bed & Breakfast

100 Harriet Isle Road, B3
St. Paul, MN 55107
(651)292-1411
www.covingtoninn.com
towboat@covingtoninn.com

Host: Liz Miller

The Covington Inn is one of America's few floating Bed & Breakfasts, buoyed and buffered as it is by the Mississippi River. Whether blanketed by snow or passed by summer's silent barges, its riverside setting soothes and captivates.

Rates at The Covington Inn Bed & Breakfast range from $140 to $235.
Rates include a full breakfast.

Blueberry Cornmeal Muffins

These are the best muffins ever! The baked blueberries complement the hearty cornmeal in a mouthwatering way. I serve them with the cheesiest scrambled eggs, fresh fruit and crispy bacon – delicious!

Serves 12

2 cups light brown sugar
2 sticks (1 cup) butter, softened
4 eggs
1/2 cup orange juice
2 Tablespoons vanilla
2 cups sifted flour
1-1/3 cups cornmeal
3 teaspoons baking powder
2 cups blueberries, fresh or frozen
sugar to sprinkle on top

2 medium mixing bowls
jumbo muffin pan for 12

Baking Time: 40-50 minutes
Baking Temperature: 375°

Preheat oven to 375°. In a medium mixing bowl, beat brown sugar and butter until smooth. Add orange juice, eggs and vanilla; beat until smooth. In a separate bowl, combine dry ingredients. Add blueberries to dry ingredients. Slowly add dry mixture to wet mixture until fully combined. Do not over mix.

Scoop batter evenly into muffin cups. Sprinkle sugar generously over tops. Bake for 40-50 minutes or until tops are golden brown.

Country Cove
Bed & Breakfast

11591 McKusick Road North
Stillwater, MN 55082
(651)430-3434
(800)646-5122
www.countrycove.com
countrycove@juno.com

Hosts: Ken & Ardie Johnson

Country Cove Bed & Breakfast is nestled in a private country setting just three minutes from downtown Stillwater. The Gateway Bike Trail is one mile away, and Sawmill and Loggers Golf Courses are at our door. The Inn has four guest rooms, each with a private bath, fireplace, TV/VCR and comfortable sitting area. A homemade country breakfast is served daily. We are handicap accessible and have a large stone fireplace in the Great Room. Meeting rooms are available. Come discover the tranquility at Country Cove.

Rates at Country Cove Bed & Breakfast range from $99 to $149.
Rates include a full breakfast.

Breakfast Puff

Our guests are delighted with our version of the Pannekokken. The fruit topping and whipped cream are attractive and enjoyed by all.

Serves 2-4 (may be doubled)

2 **eggs**
1/2 **cup milk**
1/2 **cup flour**
1/2 **teaspoon nutmeg or cinnamon**
2 **Tablespoons sugar**
4 **Tablespoons butter**

blender
9" pie plate or individual
baking dishes

Baking Time: 20-25 minutes
Baking Temperature: 425°

Preheat oven to 425°. Cut butter into 4 slices, place in pie plate and place in oven to melt. Blend ingredients slowly; add each one in order given. Pour into pie plate with melted butter. Bake for 20-25 minutes.

Toppings:
   Fresh fruit or canned pie filling
   Powdered sugar
   Whipped cream, sweetened

Sprinkle baked puff with powdered sugar. Add fruit topping and top with a generous serving of sweet whipped cream.

I usually serve this with scrambled eggs and sausage, as it is hard to bake anything else in such a hot oven.

Fruit Slush

This delicious, refreshing slush is easy to make and sure to please!

Serves 10-12

1 **package (10 ounces) frozen strawberries**
3 **bananas, cut up**
1 **can (6 ounces) frozen orange juice**
3 **cans water**
1 **can (6 ounces) frozen lemonade**
3 **cans water**
1 **cup sugar**
1 **small bottle (10 ounces) Maraschino cherries and juice**
1 **can (20 ounces) pineapple tidbits and juice**

1 **large mixing bowl**

In a large mixing bowl, mix all ingredients thoroughly and freeze. Set out 1 or 2 hours ahead of serving and chop until chunky and mushy.

Fantastic Chicken Salad

This is definitely a crowd pleaser! Try this tasty recipe at your next gathering!

Serves 10-12

2 cups cooked chicken
1 Tablespoon minced onion
1 teaspoon salt

In a large mixing bowl, combine all ingredients and refrigerate.

1 cup green grapes
1 cup chopped celery
1 cup mandarin oranges
1 cup or 1 small box macaroni rings
   (cook as directed on box)
1/2 cup cashews
1 cup mayonnaise
1 cup whipped cream or 1 small
   container (8 ounces) Cool Whip

Combine all ingredients in a large mixing bowl. Fold in whipped cream just before serving.

Historic Water Street Inn

**101 Water Street South
Stillwater, MN 55082-5150
(651)439-6000
www.waterstreetinn.us
info@waterstreetinn.us**

Hosts: Chuck & Judy Dougherty

*H*istoric Water Street Inn is in the heart of downtown Stillwater. All guest rooms have double whirlpools and most have fireplaces and balconies overlooking the St. Croix River. The restaurant has indoor and outdoor seating, and the Irish pub overlooks the river. There are meeting, banquet and wedding facilities for 2 to 300 people. The Water Street Inn is Stillwater's only hotel and restaurant on the riverfront, next to the historic lift bridge.

*Rates at Historic Water Street Inn range from $99 to $229.
Rates include a full breakfast.*

Pork Tenderloin with Red Cabbage & Maple Rum Sauce

This is a fabulous entrée that will impress the most discriminating guest!

Serves 4-5

1 pound pork tenderloin
2 teaspoons olive oil
    salt and pepper to taste

Maple Rum Sauce:
1/2 cup pure maple syrup
1/2 cup brown sugar
1/4 cup dark rum
1 Tablespoon cider vinegar
1/2 cup toasted pecans
    salt and pepper to taste
Blend until sugar is dissolved.

Red Cabbage:
8 ounces red cabbage
1/4 cup cider vinegar
1/8 cup brown sugar
Simmer until cabbage is tender.

1 medium mixing bowl
1 medium saucepan
    sauté pan

Heat sauté pan. Add oil and sear pork on all sides until brown. Slice and place on top of red cabbage. Spoon maple rum sauce over pork.

Lobster Rolls

This wonderful recipe is great for brunch or any time that you want to impress your guests!

Serves 4-5

2 ounces Julienne carrots
2 ounces Julienne onions
2 ounces shredded cabbage
1 ounce chopped spinach
8 ounces cooked lobster meat
2 Tablespoons crushed fennel
4 Tablespoons sesame oil
10 egg roll wrappers

sauté pan
deep fryer

Heat sauté pan. Add oil and carrots. Cook for 30 seconds, then add cabbage, onions and fennel. Cook for 45 seconds. Remove from heat; stir in lobster meat and spinach. Let chill.

Lay out 1 egg roll wrapper and brush each end with egg wash. Add 1 ounce of chilled filling, then wrap using the egg roll wrapping technique. Fry in 375° oil for 3-4 minutes.

Coconut Battered Shrimp with Peach Dipping Sauce

This is another great seafood recipe that will add flair to any meal!

Serves 4-5

1	pound U15 shrimp, peeled, deveined, with tail on
1	cup all-purpose flour
1	cup coconut
2	cups beer batter *(see below)*

Beer Batter:

1	cup all-purpose flour
2	teaspoons salt
1	teaspoon baking powder
1/2	teaspoon white pepper
3-1/4	cups beer
1/2	cup milk
2	large eggs

1	medium mixing bowl
1	medium saucepan
	hand mixer
	deep fryer

In a medium mixing bowl, combine flour, salt, baking powder and white pepper. Whisk in beer, milk and eggs.

Flour shrimp, dip in batter and roll in coconut. Fry in 350° vegetable oil until crispy. Serve with peach dipping sauce.

Peach Dipping Sauce:

2	cups frozen sliced peaches
1	cup sugar
1	cup water
1/4	cup parsley
1/2	cup horseradish

In a medium saucepan, combine peaches, water and sugar; bring to a boil. Puree with a hand mixer. Let chill and add parsley and horseradish.

Rivertown Inn

306 West Olive Street
Stillwater, MN 55082
(651)430-2955
www.rivertowninn.com
rivertown@rivertowninn.com

Hosts: Julie & Jeff Anderson, Lisa Lothson

The restored Rivertown Inn, perched atop downtown Stillwater, is the award-winning premier Inn of the scenic St. Croix valley and offers a Victorian escape like no other. Indulge in a lavish, chef-prepared 3-course breakfast and nightly social hour with wine and hors d'oeuvres. Each room features a fireplace and private bath with double whirlpool.

Rates at Rivertown Inn range from $175 to $325.
Rates include a full breakfast.

Ginger and Vanilla Baked Pineapple

The first part of this recipe is a little involved, but the final product is well worth the effort. Once the pineapple is ready, it is perfectly paired with a nice scoop of vanilla ice cream or a good spoonful of fresh mascarpone.

Serves 6-8

1-1/4 pounds granulated sugar
   2 quarts water plus 3/4 cup water
1-1/2 cups dark rum
  20 slices fresh root ginger, unpeeled
   4 fresh vanilla pods, split and scraped
   2 Tablespoons vanilla extract
   3 whole, peeled bananas
   1 whole pineapple, trimmed and any eyes removed

chopping board
sharp chef/kitchen knife
large, heavy bottomed pot
   (it is important that the pot is not Teflon coated and large enough for 1 whole pineapple)
   1 wooden spoon

Baking Time: 2 hours
Baking Temperature: 375°

Preheat oven to 375°

This is the hard part! But don't worry if you haven't made caramel before. In your deep pot, mix sugar with 3/4 cup water. Place over high heat. If you have an extraction fan, turn it on high. Every so often, gently move the pot in a circular motion to maintain an even temperature. If the edges of the caramel seem to be getting darker than the middle, you can brush the inside edge of the pot with cold water. Be careful, as it will spit.

Here is the fun part! When the sugar is a rich golden color, very carefully add rum – stand back as it will ignite. If it doesn't, hold a lit taper or a candle lighter into the vapors. It should light very easily.

When alcohol is burned off, add remaining ingredients. Bring to a boil, cover pot with aluminum foil and place in oven. After 1 hour, turn pineapple over and place back in oven for 1 more hour.

Transfer pineapple and liquid into a suitable container; let stand and cool for 1 hour. Then chill completely in refrigerator.

To serve, slice pineapple into 3/4" slices. Remove core by using a knife or apple corer. Pour liquid on pineapple plus your choice of topping.

Another great recipe from Rivertown Inn:

Dark Chocolate and Earl Grey Crème Brulee

This twist on the classic crème brulee introduces a fun and interesting flavor combination which works surprisingly well.

Serves 8

1/2 gallon heavy whipping cream
16 egg yolks
1-1/2 cups sugar plus sugar for topping
1 cup loose Earl Grey tea *(preferably white tip tea)*
12 ounces good quality dark chocolate *(50-70% cocoa)*, chopped finely

8 6-ounce ramekins
1 deep-sided oven pan, large enough to hold ramekins
1 large mixing bowl
1 large saucepan *(at least 3 quarts)*
1 fine sieve/strainer
1 large pitcher or bowl *(at least 1 gallon)*
1 whisk
1 ladle
1 gas torch/burner

Baking Time: 45-75 minutes
Baking Temperature: 300°

Preheat oven to 300°. Heat the cream in large saucepan until almost boiling. Turn down temperature to a very low simmer. Add tea and let it steep for 8-10 minutes.

Meanwhile, combine egg yolks and sugar in a large mixing bowl using the whisk. Add chocolate. Using the strainer, strain the hot cream onto the egg mixture. Stir until all chocolate is melted. Let mixture sit for 5 minutes.

Using the ladle, carefully skim off any foam or bubbles and strain the mixture again into a pitcher. Pour slowly into ramekins, filling each about 3/4 full. Place ramekins in pan and cover pan with aluminum foil, leaving one corner folded back.

Fill the pan with boiling water so the water reaches at least halfway up the ramekins. Fold the foil down completely, covering the pan.

Bake for 45-75 minutes or until custard appears firm. Be careful not to over bake. Remove from oven and leave in water-filled pan until cooled. Remove ramekins from water and cover with plastic wrap; refrigerate for at least 2 hours or up to 2 days.

When ready to serve, sprinkle about 2 teaspoons sugar over each custard. Use a gas torch/burner to melt sugar. Place ramekins in refrigerator for a few minutes before serving.

Lamb Cutlet with Red Onion Jam

I chose to share this recipe because I have had great reactions from not only guests but family, too. The jam is so rich and extremely versatile it pairs well with all types of meat (even burgers) and firm fish as well.

Serves 4-6

Lamb Cutlet:
- 1 **rack of lamb, Frenched**
  (bones exposed). Your butcher will trim the rack for you.
- 2 **Tablespoons vegetable oil**
- 1 **Tablespoon unsalted butter**
- 3 **sprigs rosemary**
- 3 **cloves garlic, whole and unpeeled**
-   **sea salt**
-   **ground black pepper**

- 1 **ovenproof skillet**
- 1 **chopping board**
- 1 **deep, heavy bottomed saucepan (4 quarts)**
- 1 **chef/large kitchen knife**
- 1 **wooden spoon**

Baking Time: 1 hour for jam, 20-25 minutes for lamb
Baking Temperature: 350°

Preheat oven to 350°. If there is excessive fat on the lamb, trim off desired amount; leave 1/4" for flavor. Using a sharp knife, gently score the fat, cutting in a criss-cross pattern, slightly scoring any sinew.

Heat the skillet over high heat. When pan is hot, add oil and when oil is hot, add butter, lamb (fat side down), rosemary and garlic. Brown lamb, then turn over. Place the skillet in the oven with lamb fat side up. Sprinkle with seasoning. Cook lamb until center temperature is 155° - make sure you take the temperature at the largest part of the meat. If you would like the lamb cooked medium well to well done, cook longer, until temperature is 165-170°. Remove lamb and let rest for 10 minutes.

Cut lamb by cutting in between the bones. Serve the lamb on top of the jam with your choice of potato and vegetable. I recommend sautéed or roasted baby reds and grilled asparagus. Enjoy!

Red Onion Jam:
- 2 **Tablespoons olive oil**
- 3/4 **cup cold, cubed butter – divided into 1/2 cup and 1/4 cup**
- 2 **large red onions, finely sliced**
- 2 **Tablespoons dark brown sugar**
- 1/2 **cup balsamic vinegar**
- 1 **cup red wine**
- 1 **cup port**
- 2 **cups beef stock**

Heat oil and 1/4 cup butter in deep skillet. Add onion and cook until soft over medium heat. Add brown sugar and cook for 4 minutes, stirring every so often. Add vinegar and reduce by 80% or until almost gone. One by one, repeat with wine, port and stock. When dark in color and quite thick, stir in remaining butter. Season to taste.

High Woods

35930 Wild Mountain Road
Taylors Falls, MN 55084
(651)465-5307
www.highwoods.net
highwood@frontiernet.net

Hosts: Mary Jo & Mike Mandell

High Woods is a contemporary family home located near the St. Croix River, just minutes from canoeing, boating, hiking, snowmobile and cross-country ski trails. One mile north is Wild Mountain Recreation Area, featuring water slides, go-carts, alpine slide, downhill skiing, etc. Rock climbing, bike riding, inline skating, scenic boat excursions and dinner cruises through The Dalles are all a short distance away. Or you may choose to spend a lazy afternoon tubing down the Sunrise River.

Sit back and relax in our cozy, comfy living room with wood burning fireplace, TV/VCR, games, etc. or watch your favorite movie on DSS. There are individual heat controls in all rooms and central air conditioning. We serve a full breakfast, and kitchen and grill are available for your use. A delicious plate of homemade cookies awaits your arrival plus complimentary hot and cold beverages and microwave popcorn.

There is an outdoor patio/garden area with numerous species of birds and an upper wood sundeck where you may view beautiful nesting bald eagles.

We feature a non-smoking environment and welcome children 12 and older. No pets, please.

Rates at High Woods range from $145 to $159.
Rates include a full breakfast.

Coffee Kringle

This is a quick and easy recipe that is sure to delight your guests!

Serves 8-10

Kringle:
- 1 cup water
- 1/2 cup butter or margarine
- 1/2 teaspoon almond flavoring
- 1 cup flour
- 3 eggs
  nuts, optional, and for topping

Frosting:
- 2 cups powdered sugar
- 2 Tablespoons melted butter
- 1/2 teaspoon almond flavoring
  milk, as needed

Combine all ingredients and mix thoroughly. Frost kringle when cooled.

medium saucepan
cookie sheet

Baking Time: 45 minutes
Baking Temperature: 400°

Preheat oven to 400°. In a medium saucepan, heat water and butter to boiling point. Remove from heat and add flour. Stir until smooth. Stir in eggs, one at a time, until smooth. Add almond flavoring. Add nuts, if desired.

Place by tablespoons in a ring shape on lightly greased cookie sheet. Smooth together with a knife. Bake for 45 minutes. Cool before frosting. Sprinkle with nuts, if desired.

Crazy Crust Dinners

A great quick and easy recipe – kids love it, too!

Serves 4-8

Crust:
1/2 cup flour
1/2 teaspoon salt
1/2 teaspoon baking powder
1/4 cup solid shortening
1/2 cup sour cream

1 medium mixing bowl
9" metal pie pan
sauce pan

Baking Time: 18-28 minutes
Baking Temperature: 425°

Preheat oven to 425°. Lightly grease and flour bottom and sides of pie pan. In a medium mixing bowl, combine all ingredients. Stir until blended, about 60-70 strokes. Batter will be slightly lumpy. Spread batter thinly on bottom and thickly up sides of pie pan, up to 1/4" of pan rim. Fill with one of fillings listed below and bake as directed below.

Barbecued Beef Filling:
1 pound ground beef
1/2 cup chopped green
    pepper or celery
1 Tablespoon mustard
2 teaspoons
    Worcestershire sauce

1/4 cup chopped onion
1/2 cup catsup
2 cups shredded Cheddar
    or American cheese

saucepan

Brown beef and drain, if necessary. Stir in remaining ingredients except cheese. Spoon into crust. Bake for 18-28 minutes or until crust is golden brown. Remove from oven. Sprinkle with cheese. Return to oven until cheese is melted. Cool for 5 minutes before cutting.

Italian Beef and Cheese Dinner Filling:
1 pound ground beef
1 teaspoon sage
1 teaspoon oregano
1/4 teaspoon garlic powder
1/2 cup chopped onion, if desired
1 can (6 ounces) tomato paste
1 can (4 ounces) sliced mushrooms plus juice

Brown beef and drain, if necessary. Stir in remaining ingredients. Spoon into crust. Bake for 18-28 minutes or until crust is golden brown. Cool for 5 minutes before cutting.

Rhubarb Crunch

This is a great recipe for when rhubarb is in season. It's quick and easy, too!

Serves 8-10

    1   box yellow cake mix
    2   cups granulated sugar
    5   cups rhubarb
    4   Tablespoons flour
    1   egg
1-1/2   sticks (3/4 cup) butter or margarine

    1   large mixing bowl
        9" x 12" baking pan

        Baking Time: 1 hour
        Baking Temperature: 350°

Preheat oven to 350°. Prepare cake mix according to box directions. Set aside. In a large mixing bowl, combine sugar, rhubarb, flour and egg. Mix thoroughly and spread in a greased baking pan. Spread cake mix over top. Crumble butter and sprinkle over entire mixture. Bake for 1 hour.

The Log House & Homestead

44854 Fredholm Road
P.O. Box 130
Vergas, MN 56587
(218)342-2318
(800)342-2318
www.loghousebb.com
loghouse@tekstar.com

Host: Suzanne Tweten

The Log House & Homestead on Spirit Lake is cradled amidst 115 acres of hills, fields and maple woods, adjacent to almost a mile of wooded shore. Luxury, pampering and privacy are its hallmark. It is a one-of-a-kind Bed & Breakfast, combining the beauty and peacefulness of the land with luxurious amenities and personal attention. Although it is a great "getaway" location, a wide range of area activities and events are easily accessible.

While the Inn's beautiful furnishings and luxurious amenities, including whirlpools, fireplaces, fine linens and fresh flowers, will make your stay memorable, our breakfasts will make your stay unforgettable. We put great emphasis on the "direct from grower or producer to table" concept. We grow our own produce or buy locally whenever we can. We use only Fair Trade organic coffees and teas.

Rates at The Log House & Homestead range from $110 to $215.
Rates include a full breakfast.

Bacon Crepes Florentine

This is a somewhat time-consuming recipe but well worth the effort! Our guest rave about it, and it saves time in the morning because it is prepared the evening before. This elegant dish has a beautiful presentation. We serve it with popovers and wild fruit preserves made from fruit from our own land. No meat is required. Fresh pineapple with mango coulis or baked sherried grapefruit make a delicious accompaniment.

Makes 4 servings

Crepes:
1/2 cup plus 2 Tablespoons water
1/2 cup milk
 3 large eggs
 2 Tablespoons melted butter
1/2 teaspoon salt
 1 cup flour
1/2 cup parsley sprigs

Filling:
 1 pound bacon, cut into
    1" pieces
 1 package (8 ounces) sliced
    mushrooms
 2 packages (10 ounces each)
    frozen spinach, thawed
 6 green onions, thinly sliced,
    keep green stems
 1 Tablespoon butter
 4 Tablespoons flour
 1 cup milk

Sauce:
3/4 cup water
3/4 cup white wine
 1 chicken bullion cube
 2 Tablespoons chopped shallots
 2 Tablespoons white wine
    vinegar
 3 Tablespoons butter
Mix all ingredients except butter in a small saucepan and bring to a boil. Reduce to half. Swirl in butter.

   food processor
 1 medium mixing bowl
 1 large mixing bowl
   crepe pan
   sauté pan
   cookie sheet
   small saucepan

Baking Time: 20-25 minutes
Baking Temperature: 250°

Crepes:

Place all ingredients in a food processor. Process for 5-10 seconds, then scrape down sides. Process for 20 seconds. Pour into a medium mixing bowl and refrigerate for at least 4 hours or overnight.

Preheat a crepe pan on medium heat until hot but not smoking. Use a scant 1/4 cup batter for each crepe. Rotate pan quickly to evenly spread batter. Fry for approximately 1 minute, then flip to other side and fry for about 50 seconds.

Remove crepe from pan and place on wax paper, layering wax paper between each crepe (makes 10-12 crepes). Crepes may be made the day before and wrapped in plastic.

Filling:

Fry bacon until crisp. Use a slotted spoon to place bacon on paper toweling to drain. In the same pan, sauté mushrooms. Place in a large mixing bowl. In

continued...

... Bacon Crepes Florentine continued:

same pan, sauté green onions, including green stem. Add spinach and cook until most liquid is gone. Stir in butter and sprinkle mixture with flour, stirring until incorporated. Add milk all at once. Stir until thickened. Add to mushrooms and mix well. Stir in bacon.

Assembling crepes:

Preheat oven to 250°. Fill crepes one at a time. Place 1/4 cup filling on one quadrant of each crepe. Fold crepe in half over the filling and fold in half again to form a triangle. Place finished crepes on lightly buttered cookie sheet. Cover with aluminum foil and warm in oven for 20-25 minutes.

Place 2 crepes on each warmed serving plate and drizzle 2-3 Tablespoons of sauce on crepes. Garnish with a sprig of parsley and serve immediately.

Another great recipe from The Log House & Homestead:

Peach Compote with Basil

This delicate fruit dish goes beautifully with all non-sweet entrees. Its subtle flavor and creamy texture make it a particularly elegant first course.

Makes 4 servings

5-6	white peaches, sliced and peeled
1	cup water
1/2	cup sugar
4	teaspoons butter, cut into pieces
1/2	cup fresh basil
1/2	teaspoon vanilla

medium saucepan

In saucepan, combine sugar and water. Stir over medium heat until sugar dissolves. Add peaches and simmer for 2 minutes. Add butter, stirring until melted. Add basil and cook until wilted, about 30 seconds. Stir in vanilla.

Serve at room temperature.

Bette Noir (Decadent Flourless Cake)

Guests always find this delicious, decadent dessert on their welcome trays. It is accompanied by fruit, cheese, crackers and non-alcoholic wine. Crystal, china, silver and linen napkins on a wooden tray complete this elegant presentation.

Makes 16 servings

- 8 ounces Baker's unsweetened chocolate
- 4 ounces quality bittersweet chocolate
- 1/2 cup water
- 1-1/3 cups sugar
- 2 sticks (1 cup) butter , cut into pieces
- 5 extra large eggs

All ingredients should be at room temperature.

9" round cake pan
medium saucepan
larger pan to set round cake pan into
cookie sheet

Baking Time: 25-30 minutes
Baking Temperature: 350°

Preheat oven to 350° with rack in center of oven. Butter cake pan and place a circle of parchment or wax paper on the bottom. Butter the paper.

Coarsely chop both chocolates and set aside. In saucepan, combine water and sugar and bring to a boil. Continue boiling for 2 minutes, stirring with a wooden spoon. Remove from heat and immediately add chocolate pieces, stirring until completely melted. Add butter, piece by piece, stirring until completely melted. Add eggs one at a time, beating each only until incorporated. Do not over beat.

Gently spoon and scrape the mixture into prepared pan. Place pan in larger pan and pour hot water into the larger pan until water cover reaches half the height of the cake pan. Bake for 25-30 minutes or until toothpick inserted in center comes out moist. Cool cake for 10 minutes.

Run a knife around pan to release. Cover with cookie sheet. Invert pan. Place a serving plate over the cake and flip it over. Wrap well with foil or plastic wrap and chill overnight.

Pine Cone
Bed & Breakfast

522 2nd Avenue Northeast
Waseca, MN 56093
(507)835-5863
(800)930-CONE
Pinecone@hickorytech.net

Hosts: Linda and Charles Cone

This historic landmark home is on the National Register of Historic Places. Built in 1895 and purchased in 1900 by merchant and businessman W.R. Wolf, this Queen Anne Victorian is decorated to reflect the Victorian era, with an ornate fireplace and an open oak staircase that leads to four guest rooms on the second floor. Each room has a private bathroom.

Waseca has two lakes within the city limits. There are antique shops, gourmet coffee shops and historic buildings. We are 15 minutes from Cabela's Sporting Goods Center and minutes from Farm America.

Rates at Pine Cone Bed & Breakfast range from $65 to $115.
Rates include a full breakfast.

Granny Smith Apple French Toast

Prepare this recipe the night before and impress your guests with this delicious breakfast entrée!

Serves 6

4 Granny Smith apples or other good baking apples	1 small mixing bowl
1/2 cup water	1 large mixing bowl
1 teaspoon cinnamon	9" x 13" baking pan
1-2 Tablespoons sugar, to taste	skillet
3/4 cup brown sugar	
3 Tablespoons light corn syrup	Baking Time: 40 minutes
3 Tablespoons butter or margarine	Baking Temperature: 325°
1/2 cup chopped pecans	
12 slices firm white bread	
3 eggs	
1-1/4 cups milk	
1 teaspoon vanilla	
1/4 teaspoon nutmeg	

Peel, core and slice apples. Place in skillet. Pour water over apples. Simmer 4-5 minutes or until tender. Drain apples. Place in a large mixing bowl and gently mix in cinnamon and sugar. Set aside.

In same skillet, combine brown sugar, corn syrup and butter. Cook and stir over medium heat until sugar melts and mixture just comes to a boil. Pour into baking pan. Sprinkle with nuts. Place 6 bread slices on top of syrup and nuts. Spread apples over bread and top with remaining 6 bread slices.

In a small mixing bowl, whisk together eggs, milk, vanilla and nutmeg. Pour over top of bread and apples. Cover and refrigerate overnight.

In the morning, preheat oven to 325°. Bake uncovered for 40 minutes. Serve each piece inverted on a plate. Cut diagonally and serve with warm vanilla sauce.

Vanilla Sauce:
- 1/2 cup sugar
- 1 Tablespoon cornstarch
- 1 cup water
- 2 Tablespoons butter or margarine
- 1 Tablespoon vanilla

Mix sugar, cornstarch and water in saucepan. Cook, stirring often, over medium heat until thick and bubbly. Remove from heat; add butter and vanilla. Stir until butter melts. Pour over French toast.

Windom Park
Bed & Breakfast

369 West Broadway
Winona, MN 55987
(507)457-9515
(866)737-1719
www.windompark.com

Hosts: Craig & Karen Groth, Mary Koontz

Enjoy the quiet charm of our handsome Colonial Revival home. Built in 1900 by a prominent Winona banker, our Inn is located in one of Winona's historic neighborhoods, across the street from a Victorian park. Classic details, mellow woods and large fireplaces with marble and quarter-sawn oak create the perfect setting for an escape into the more genteel past. For 27 years, we have enjoyed B&Bs throughout the United States and England with the hope of one day owning our own. Now, let us share our experiences with you by offering you an American B&B with an English accent in the historic river town of Winona. Our celebrated five-course breakfast is served in the formal dining room. We offer evening wine and cheese in the Great Room or backyard, depending upon the weather. We have three rooms and one suite in the main house. There are two rooms in the Coach House, with in-room Jacuzzis and fireplaces. All rooms have private baths. Come stay with us and take home a memory.

Rates at Windom Park Bed & Breakfast range from $99 to $175.
Rates include a full breakfast.

Craig's Baked Cinnamon Apple French Toast

This recipe is Craig's specialty and has become our signature dish. It should be put together the night before to allow bread to soak up the egg mixture. We have books in our guest room and get constant thumbs up about this dish. Served with fresh fruit and bacon, it is a magnificent breakfast or brunch offering.

Serves 8-10

1 cup firmly packed brown sugar
1/2 cup butter or margarine
2 Tablespoons light corn syrup
3 large apples *(Craig uses Braeburns)*,
      peeled, cored and sliced day-
      old French bread sliced into
      3/4" slices
3 eggs
1 cup milk
1 Tablespoon vanilla extract
   ground cinnamon

1 large mixing bowl
   9" x 13" baking dish
   small saucepan

Baking Time: 35-40 minutes
Baking Temperature: 350°

In a small saucepan, combine brown sugar, butter and corn syrup until thick, about 2-3 minutes. Immediately pour into ungreased baking dish, making sure bottom is evenly covered. Arrange apple slices, overlapping, on top of brown sugar mixture.

In a large bowl, beat eggs, milk and vanilla. Dip the bread slices in the egg mixture, allowing them to soak for 30 seconds. Arrange bread on top of apples and pour remaining egg mixture over bread. Sprinkle generously with cinnamon. Cover and refrigerate overnight.

In the morning, remove from refrigerator and let sit for 30 minutes at room temperature. Preheat oven to 350°.

Bake for 35-40 minutes. Cut into slices and place on plates; spoon some of the syrup over the French toast.

Bridget's Irish Scones

Our best friend in Chicago was our neighbor Bridget. She came from Ireland when she was 16 years old and brought with her many wonderful recipes. The scones are light and melt in your mouth; the secret is the sour cream. Our guests ask for the scone recipe more than anything else that we serve. This is an easy recipe to half, if desired.

Makes about 4 dozen scones

4 cups flour
2 teaspoons baking powder
1 teaspoon baking soda
1/2 teaspoon salt
1 cup sugar
1/2 cup (1 stick) butter or margarine, cut into small cubes (keep cold)
2 cups raisins, currants, dried cranberries or any other small dried fruit
1 pint (16 ounces) sour cream
2 eggs

1 small mixing bowl
1 large mixing bowl
cookie sheet(s)

Baking Time: 10-12 minutes
Baking Temperature: 400°

Preheat oven to 400°. Put all dry ingredients except fruit in a large mixing bowl and thoroughly mix together with your fingers. Mix butter cubes into dry ingredients with fingers until thoroughly incorporated; the mixture should have a mealy texture. Add dried fruit to mixture and incorporate with your fingers.

In a small mixing bowl, combine sour cream and eggs until blended. Make a well in the middle of the dry ingredients and pour egg mixture in. With a spoon, blend together until all dry ingredients are moist. The dough will be very sticky.

Drop generous teaspoons of dough onto a greased cookie sheet. You may need another spoon or spatula to push dough off spoon. Space about 1-1/2" apart.

Bake for 10-12 minutes or until golden brown. Serve with freshly whipped cream and the fruit preserve of your choice.

Karen's Greek Style Crostini

We serve wine and cheese to our guests in the early evening. As our list of return guests grows, I have experimented with various appetizers so there is some variation in what we are serving. Although crostini is Italian in origin, this recipe reflects our love of anything Greek. It is easy to make, and our guests have given it rave reviews.

Makes 24-30 finished crostini

Topping:
1 jar Peloponnese brand sun-dried tomato relish, *available in most grocery stores in their international food section*
2 Roma tomatoes, seeded and chopped
1 container (4 ounces) crumbled Feta cheese
12 Kalamata olives, pitted and chopped coarsely
1/4 cup chopped arugula or Italian parsley

1 large mixing bowl
cookie sheet(s)
decorative plate and bowl for serving

Baking Time: 7-10 minutes
Baking Temperature: 450°

Topping Preparation:
In a large mixing bowl, mix all ingredients together early in the day and refrigerate so flavors blend. May be refrigerated for 3-4 days.

Crostini:
There are a variety of brands that can be bought commercially, but I like the flavor of homemade crostini better.

To make at home, you'll need:
• One or more narrow French baguette, cut into 1/4" slices, cutting at a slight angle.
• Olive oil
• Powdered garlic
Brush both sides of bread with olive oil; sprinkle with garlic. Place on cookie sheet in a preheated 450° oven and bake until golden on one side, then turn and toast other side, with a total cooking time of 7-10 minutes. Cool completely and store crostini in a plastic bag until ready to use. They will keep for 2-3 days.

To serve:
Put tomato mixture in bowl set on a large plate surrounded by crostini and let guests help themselves. For a more formal occasion, place a spoonful of the tomato mixture on each crostini and arrange on a large plate.

The Barteau House
Bed & Breakfast

10 Jefferson Drive
P.O. Box 51
Zumbrota, MN 55992
(507)732-4466
(866)227-8328
www.barteauhouse.com
info@barteauhouse.com

Hosts: Scott & Kim Jensen

Built in 1895 for Sidney B. Barteau, proprietor of hardware and farm supply stores, this elegant Queen Anne Victorian has been lovingly restored to its original splendor. Nestled in the trees on just over four acres, our grounds create an enchanting hideaway, including wraparound front porch, gazebo, fountain, fish pond and walking paths. We offer four beautifully appointed guest rooms, all with private baths, queen-size beds and fireplaces. Some rooms have whirlpool tubs. Awaken to the aroma of freshly brewed coffee and enjoy a full, candlelight breakfast served in our dining room. We are minutes away from golfing, canoeing, bike trails, downhill and cross-country skiing, shopping and fine dining.

Rates at The Barteau House Bed & Breakfast range from $89 to $149.
Rates include a full breakfast.

Crab Quiche Bake

Colorful, delicious and easy! I usually chop all the ingredients the night before and mix and bake in the morning. We serve this quiche with oven roasted herb potatoes and coffee cake. Our guests enjoy this satisfying, tasty dish.

Makes 8 servings

8   eggs, beaten
2   cups half-and-half cream
1   large sweet red pepper, chopped
1   package (8 ounces) imitation (or real)
     crabmeat, chopped
1   cup soft bread crumbs
1   cup shredded Swiss cheese
1   cup shredded Cheddar cheese
1/2   cup chopped green onions
1   teaspoon salt
1/2   teaspoon pepper

1   large mixing bowl
     13" x 9" x 2" baking dish

Baking Time: 30-35 minutes
Baking Temperature: 350°

Preheat oven to 350°. In a large mixing bowl, combine all ingredients. Transfer to a greased baking dish.

Bake, uncovered, for 30-35 minutes or until a knife inserted near center comes out clean.

Let stand 10 minutes before serving.

Helpful Tips for the Cook

- When grating lemon peel, take care to not include the bitter white layer.

- Chocolate can be melted easily by grating it and placing it in an ovenware dish in a 325° oven. Watch it carefully and remove when the proper consistency is reached.

- Cutting boards are bacteria-friendly. After use, wash the board with a mild soap and rub the surface with fresh lemon juice.

- Don't overlook the steaming method of preparing vegetables. Steaming is a great way to preserve the nutrient value of the food as well as the flavor.

- Grated Mozzarella cheese is a handy staple. Buy the cheese in quantity and grate it. Add a tad of cornstarch and toss well. Enjoy using grated cheese that does not clump together.

- A pinch of salt added to an egg-wash will improve the appearance of pie crust.

- Leftover egg yolks can be stored in water in the refrigerator and used at a later time.

- Bring out the flavor of nuts by warming them briefly in a slow oven to bring out the natural oils.

- Brush the sides of the saucepan with oil before heating milk to prevent the milk from foaming up.

- Add 1 teaspoon of oil to the water used for cooking pasta and prevent bubbling over.

- Use a coffee grinder to grind herbs. Then grind a crust of bread to clean the grinder.

- Add a slice of bread to a bag of hardened brown sugar and restore it to a usable state.

- If a recipe calls for honey and oil, use the same cup, measuring out the oil first; then the honey. The honey will not adhere to the sides and bottom of the cup.

- Add garlic flakes to containers used to store grains. Insects will be repelled.

- Soak hard-boiled eggs in ice water for at least 5 minutes after cooking for ease in removing shells.

- Add a dash of horseradish to mashed potatoes to give them a "lift."

- Celery will keep longer if it is wrapped in foil.

Notes

Directory of
Minnesota Bed & Breakfast Association Membership

Bold type: Inns listed in this book.

City	Inn	Phone	Website Address
Afton	Afton House Inn	651-436-8883	www.aftonhouseinn.com
Alexandria	**Cedar Rose Inn**	**888-203-5333**	**www.cedarroseinn.com**
	Lake Le Homme Dieu Bed & Breakfast	320-846-5875	www.llbedandbreakfast.com
	Sweet Retreat	320-283-6050	www.sweetretreatbandb.com
Annandale	Thayer's Historic Bed N' Breakfast	320-274-8222	www.thayers.net
Anoka	**Ticknor Hill Bed & Breakfast**	**800-484-3954 x6391**	**www.ticknorhill.com**
Ashby	Harvest Inn	218-747-2334	www.harvestinn.net
Battle Lake	**Xanadu Island Bed & Breakfast & Resort**	**800-396-9043**	**www.xanadu.cc**
Baudette	Wildwood Inn Bed & Breakfast	888-212-7031	www.wildwoodinnbb.com
Brainerd	**Whiteley Creek Homestead**	**218-829-0654**	**www.whiteleycreek.com**
Cannon Falls	**Quill & Quilt B & B**	**800-488-3849**	**www.quillandquilt.com**
Center City	**Summit Inn Bed & Breakfast**	**651-257-4987**	**www.summitinn.us**
Chaska	Bluff Creek Bed & Breakfast	800-445-6958	www.bluffcreekbb.com
	The Peacock Inn	952-368-4343	www.peacockinn.net
Chatfield	Oakenwald Terrace B&B	507-867-3806	www.oakenwaldterrace.com
Cold Spring	The Pillar Inn	320-685-3828	
Crosby	Nordic Inn	218-546-8299	www.vikinginn.com
Dexter	Ice Haus Bed & Breakfast	888-ICE-HAUS	www.icehaus.com
Duluth	A. Charles Weiss Inn (A return to Victorian Duluth)	800-525-5243	www.duluth.com/acw
	A.G. Thomson House	**218-724-3464**	**www.thomsonhouse.biz**
	Cotton Mansion	218-724-6405	www.cottonmansion.com
	Ellery House	**800-355-3794**	**www.elleryhouse.com**
	Immigrant House B&B Inn	877-724-3090	www.immigranthouse.com
	Manor on the Creek Inn/Bed & Breakfast	**800-428-3189**	**www.manoronthecreek.com**
	Mathew S. Burrows 1890 Inn B&B	**800-789-1890**	**www.1890inn.com**
	Olcott House B&B	**218-728-1339**	**www.olcotthouse.com**
	Solglimt on the Water	**877-727-0596**	**www.solglimt.com**
	The Firelight Inn on Oregon Creek	**888-724-0273**	**www.firelightinn.com**
Dundas	Archibald Inn	612-703-4149	www.archibaldinn.com
Ely	**Blue Heron B & B**	**218-365-4720**	**www.blueheronbnb.com**
Eyota	Clara-Marie B & B	507-545-2195	www.clara-marie.com
Farmington	**Akin House Bed and Breakfast**	**651-463-1298**	**www.akinhouse.com**
Fergus Falls	**Bakketopp Hus**	**800-739-2915**	**www.bbonline.com/mn/bakketopp**

City	Inn	Phone	Website Address
Finlayson	Giese Bed & Breakfast Inn	320-233-6429	www.giese-bnb.com
Foley	The Nutcracker B & B	320-387-2431	www.nutcracker-bb.com
Frazee	Acorn Lake Bed and Breakfast	218-334-5545	www.detroitlakes.com/acornlake
Grand Marais	Bally's Bed & Breakfast	218-387-1817	
	Dream Catcher Bed & Breakfast	218-387-2876	www.dreamcatcherbb.com
	Jagerhaus German B&B	877-387-1476	www.jagerhaus.com
	MacArthur House Bed & Breakfast	800-792-1840	www.macarthurhouse.com
	Pincushion Mountain Bed & Breakfast	800-542-1226	www.pincushionbb.com
	Poplar Creek Guesthouse Bed & Breakfast	**218-388-4487**	**www.littleollielodging.com**
Grand Rapids	**Morning Glory Bed & Breakfast**	**866-926-3978**	**www.morningglorybandb.com**
Harmony	Gourmets' Garden Bed & Breakfast	507-886-2971	www.gourmetsgardenbandb.com
Harris	Soleil Levant Bed & Breakfast Inn	651-674-7361	
Hastings	**Classic Rosewood & Thorwood**	**888-846-7966**	**www.thorwoodinn.com**
Henderson	Henderson House	507-248-3356	
Hendricks	Triple L Farm Bed & Breakfast	507-275-3740	
Hibbing	Mitchell-Tappan House	888-662-3862	
Hinckley	Dakota Lodge Bed & Breakfast	320-384-6052	www.dakotalodge.com
	Woodland Trails Bed & Breakfast	320-655-3901	www.woodlandtrails.net
Houston	Addie's Attic	507-896-3010	www.bluffcountry.com/addies.htm
Ivanhoe	Weaver's Haus Bed & Breakfast	507-694-1637	
Janesville	Fenelon Place	507-234-5705	www.fenelonplace.com
Jordan	**Nicolin Mansion B & B**	**952-492-6441**	**www.nicolinmansion.com**
Kenyon	Dancing Winds Farmstay Retreat	507-789-6606	www.dancingwinds.com
Lake Benton	Benton House	507-368-9484	http://hercules.itctel.com/~bentonhs/
Lake City	**Red Gables Inn Bed & Breakfast**	**651-345-2605**	**www.redgablesinn.com**
	The Frog and the Bear Bed and Breakfast	651-345-2122	www.thefrogandbear.com
Lanesboro	Berwood Hill Inn		www.berwood.com
	Habberstad House Bed & Breakfast	507-467-3560	www.habberstadhouse.com
	Hillcrest Hide-Away Bed & Breakfast	**507-467-3079**	**www.hillcresthideaway.com**
	Historic Scanlan House Bed & Breakfast	**800-944-2158**	**www.scanlanhouse.com**
	Mrs. B's Historic Lanesboro Inn & Restaurant	507-467-2154	www.mrsbsinn.com
	Scandinavian Inn	507-467-4500	www.scandinavianinn.com
	Stone Mill Suites	866-897-8663	www.stonemillsuites.com
Litchfield	Marshall Estate	320-593-8170	www.litch.com
Little Falls	The Waller House	320-632-1066	
Luverne	Our House Bed & Breakfast	888-283-9340	www.ourhousebedandbreakfast.com
Mankato	Butler House Bed & Breakfast	507-387-5055	www.butlerhouse.com

City	Inn	Phone	Website Address
Marine on St. Croix	Asa Parker House	651-433-5248	www.asaparkerbb.com
Marshall	Arbor Inn Bed & Breakfast	507-532-2457	www.arborinnbb.com
Mentor	The Inn at Maple Crossing	218-637-6600	www.innatmaplecrossing.com
Monticello	**The Historic Rand House**	**888-295-0881**	**www.randhouse.com**
Montrose	Nature's Nest	763-972-6891	www.naturesnestfarm.com
Nevis	Park Street Inn	800-797-1778	www.parkstreetinn.com
New Ulm	**Deutsche Strasse (German Street) B & B**	**866-226-9856**	**www.deutschestrasse.com**
	The Bohemian Bed & Breakfast	507-354-2268	www.the-bohemian.com
New York Mills	Whistle Stop Inn	218-385-2223	www.whistlestopbedandbreakfast.com
Northfield	The Magic Door	507-664-9096	www.magicdoorbb.com
Orr	**Hundred Acre Woods Bed & Breakfast**	**218-757-0070**	
Osage	LadySlipper Inn	800-531-2787	www.ladyslipperinn.com
Owatonna	Northrop Oftedahl House B&B	507-451-4040	www.northrop-oftedahl.com
Park Rapids	Heartland Trail B & B	218-732-3252	www.heartlandbb.com
	LoonSong Bed & Breakfast	**888-825-8135**	**www.bbhost.com/loonsongbnb**
Paynesville	Huntington House	320-243-3905	www.huntingtonhousebb.com
Pelican Rapids	**Prairie View Estate**	**800-298-8058**	**www.prairieviewestate.com**
Perham	Cathedral In the Pines	218-346-3253	www.cathedralinthepinesbb.com
Preston	Jailhouse Inn	507-765-2181	www.jailhouseinn.com
Princeton	Rum River Country Bed & Breakfast	763-389-2679	
Red Wing	Golden Lantern Inn	888-288-3315	www.goldenlantern.com
	Hungry Point Inn	651-437-3660	www.hungrypointinn.com
	Moondance Inn	866-388-8145	www.moondanceinn.com
	The Candlelight Inn	**800-254-9194**	**www.candlelightinn-redwing.com**
	The Octagon House	651-388-1778	www.octagon-house.com
Rushford	Meadows Inn Bed & Breakfast	(507) 864-2378	www.meadowsinn.com
Sanborn	Sod House on the Prairie	507-723-5138	www.sodhouse.org
Sherburn	Four Columns Inn	507-764-8861	www.fourcolumnsinn.net
Silver Bay	Baptism River Inn	877-353-0707	www.baptismriverinn.com
	Inn at Palisade on Superior	218-226-0200	www.innatpalisade.com
Sleepy Eye	W.W. Smith Inn	507-794-5661	
Spicer	Spicer Castle Inn	800-821-6675	www.spicercastle.com
Spring Valley	Somewhere in Time Bed & Breakfast	507-346-1940	
St. Cloud	Heritage House Bed & Breakfast	888-547-4422	www.heritagehousebbmn.com
	Riverside Guest Haus	888-252-2134	www.riversideguesthaus.com
	Victorian Oaks Bed & Breakfast	866-VIC-OAKS	www.vicoaks.com

City	Inn	Phone	Website Address
St. Paul	Cathedral Hill B&B	866-280-6198	www.bbonthehill.com
	Chatsworth Bed & Breakfast	**877-978-4837**	**www.chatsworth-bb.com**
	Covington Inn	**651-292-1411**	**www.covingtoninn.com**
	Crystal Dreams B&B at the Wynne Inne	651-644-7447	www.wynneinne.com
Starbuck	Berries & Marigolds	320-239-4868	www.berriesandmarigolds.com
Stillwater	Ann Bean Mansion	651-430-0355	www.annbeanmansion.com
	Aurora Staples Inn	800-580-3092	www.aurorastaplesinn.com
	Brunswick Inn	651-430-8111	www.brunswickinnstillwater.com
	Country Cove Bed & Breakfast	**800-646-5122**	**www.countrycove.com**
	James A. Mulvey Residence Inn	800-820-8008	www.jamesmulveyinn.com
	River Town Inn	**651-430-2955**	**www.rivertowninn.com**
	The Elephant Walk	888-430-0359	www.elephantwalkbb.com
	The Outing Lodge	800-439-4330	www.outinglodge.com
	The William Sauntry Mansion	800-828-2653	www.sauntrymansion.com
	Water Street Inn	**651-439-6000**	**www.waterstreetinn.us**
Taylors Falls	Country Bed & Breakfast	651-257-4773	www.countrybedandbreakfast.us
	High Woods B&B	**651-465-5307**	**www.highwoods.net**
	The Cottage Bed & Breakfast	651-465-3595	www.the-cottage.com
Truman	The Whittler's Lady B & B	507-776-8555	www.thewhittlerslady.com
Two Harbors	Lighthouse Bed & Breakfast	888-832-5606	www.lighthousebb.org
Underwood	Aloft in the Pines	888-457-6301	www.bbonline.com/mn/aloft/
Vergas	Homestead Inn	218-342-2141	www.homesteadinnmn.com
	Log House & Homestead on Spirit Lake	**800-342-2318**	**www.loghousebb.com**
Wabasha	Bridgewaters Bed & Breakfast	888-565-4201	www.bridgewatersbandb.com
	Eagles on the River Bed & Breakfast & Suites	651-565-3509	www.eaglesontheriver.com
Walker	Embracing Pines	218-224-3519	www.embracingpines.com
Waseca	**Pine Cone Bed & Breakfast**	**800-930-CONE**	
Winona	Carriage House Bed & Breakfast	507-452-8256	www.chbb.com
	Windom Park Bed & Breakfast	**866-737-1719**	**www.windompark.com**
Worthington	Historic Dayton House	507-727-1311	www.daytonhouse.org
Zumbro Falls	Burr Oaks	507-753-3133	www.burroaks.com
Zumbrota	**The Barteau House Bed & Breakfast**	**507-732-4466**	**www.barteauhouse.com**

Index of Recipes

C

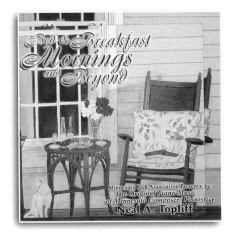

CD Companion to the Cookbook,

more senses enticed.

All the senses are inspired and treated at a B & B. One might expect soft calming soothing music. One might enjoy an innkeeper's personal concert played on a parlor piano. Or a talented guest may enjoy "trying out" the inn's keyboard.

We have been lucky here in Minnesota to discover a local musical talent---- Neal A.Topliff. Neal was born in Duluth and now resides with his family in Red Wing. Neal complimented an innkeepers' conference luncheon recently with his original music. Innkeepers were impressed and anxious to share his soothing tunes at their inns. This camaraderie has blossomed into an original selection of Neal's compositions to compliment the inn experience and specifically this travel guide/cookbook. Don't be surprised to hear Neal's fine music at your next Minnesota B & B getaway from the original CD, "Minnesota Mornings and Beyond." This CD is a collection of soul stirring solo piano pieces.

Neal's music is personal, heartfelt and has a hint of nostalgia. With song titles such as, "Coming Home", " Sunset for Two", "Peaceful Hideaway" and "Same Time Next Year", this 15 song CD is sure to take you on a peaceful journey where you come away feeling soothed, relaxed and refreshed! Neal is the owner of Harbour Light Music. His music has been featured on radio stations and television programs around the country including MPR's Morning Show, Venture North, Almanac and the Kare 11 Morning Show. Now he plays for you at your favorite B & B as well as in your home with this fine CD designed to accompany the inn experience.

To order the cookbook and CD package, contact the MBBA at 651-438-7499 or info@minnesotabedandbreakfasts.org. Or visit the website and order directly. www.minnesotabedandbreakfasts.org. The CD may be ordered by itself as well. Wholesale information is also available. The cookbook and CD will also be for sale at MBBA member inns.

Minnesota
Bed & Breakfast
Association

To order additional copies of
More Minnesota Mornings and Beyond-
A Cookbook & Travel Guide

as well as other books in the Bed & Breakfast
series or for a FREE catalog contact The Guest
Cottage Inc. Also, visit us online at
www.theguestcottage.com

The
Guest
Cottage Inc.
dba Amherst Press

PO Box 848
Woodruff, WI 54568
voice: 800-333-8122
fax: 715-358-9456